Copyright © Wes Lambert

The moral rights of the author have been asserted.

All rights reserved. No part of this book may be reproduced, stored in a retrieval system, communicated or transmitted in any form or by any means without prior written permission.

All enquiries should be made to the author.

Saving Hospitality, One Venue at a Time - The 7 Pillars to Pivoting Your Business Through a Crisis

ISBN: 978-0-6488788-0-3

Disclaimer

The material in this publication is of the nature of general comment only, and does not represent professional advice. It is not intended to provide specific guidance for particular circumstances and it should not be relied on as the basis for any decision to take action or not take action on any matter which it covers.

Readers should obtain professional advice where appropriate, before making any such decision. To the maximum extent permitted by law, the author and publisher disclaim all responsibility and liability to any person, arising directly or indirectly from any person taking or not taking action based on the information in this publication.

For Grace

# Saving Hospitality, One Venue at a Time

## The 7 Pillars to Pivoting Your Business Through a Crisis

Wes Lambert

# *Table of Contents*

Acknowledgements ................................................................... 1
Introduction & Testimonials ....................................................... 2
Chapter One - Becoming a Hospitality Champion ....................... 5
    The Perfect Storm ................................................................ 8
    What You Will Discover in This Book ................................ 11
Chapter Two - Introducing the 7 Pillars of a Successful Pivot ..... 12
    What Are the 7 Pillars to Pivoting? .................................... 14
Chapter Three - Pillar #1 – Find a Trusted Mentor ..................... 15
    You Don't Know What You Don't Know .......................... 17
    5 Reasons Why a Mentor Is Critical to Success ................. 18
    The Traits of a Great Mentor ............................................. 21
    Find the Guidance You Need ............................................. 28
Chapter Four - Pillar #2 – Understand Your Financials .............. 29
    The Numbers Don't Lie ..................................................... 31
    What Is Your Break-Even Point? ....................................... 32
    Create Regular Profit and Loss (P&L) Statements ............. 34
    Penny Profit vs. Cost ......................................................... 39
    Menu Engineering ............................................................. 40
    Stay on Top of Your Numbers ........................................... 42
Chapter Five - Pillar #3 – Create a Forecast to Predict the Future ........ 43
    Five Reasons Why Forecasting Is Critical for Success ...... 45
    Steps to Creating a Sales Forecast ..................................... 48
    10 Tips for Creating Accurate Forecasts ............................ 52
    Prepare for the Future ........................................................ 57
Chapter Six - Pillar #4 – Make a Plan (and Measure Against It) ........ 58
    Creating Your Plan – The Key Steps ................................. 61
    Developing a Marketing Plan ............................................ 67

Be the Jet Engine (Not the Propeller)..................................................73

Prepare for Changes..................................................................................75

Chapter Seven - Pillar #5 – Create New Streams of Revenue...............76

Other Streams of Revenue to Consider ........................................78

Maximise Your Revenue Potential................................................86

Chapter Eight - Pillar #6 – Execute the Plan..........................................87

10 Tips for Getting Buy-In from Your Employees .....................89

How to Execute Your New plan.....................................................95

Take Massive Action.......................................................................99

Chapter Nine - Pillar #7 – Continue to Pivot and
Make Changes Where Necessary ..........................................................100

Don't Be Afraid to Throw in the Towel ....................................104

Embrace Failure............................................................................111

Chapter Ten - It's Time to Make a Change..........................................112

The Future Is in Your Hands ......................................................113

Learn to Appreciate Failure........................................................114

Choose Your People Wisely.........................................................115

Get to Know Your Business ........................................................116

Don't Stop Evolving......................................................................117

Resources ..................................................................................................118

# *Acknowledgements*

I would like to give a heartfelt thank you and commend:

All the hospitality business owners who push through challenges and crises to bring the highest quality service, food and beverage to diners throughout Australia and the world.

The entire R&CA Team for everything you do, every single day, especially Bel & Tom, my right and left hands.

The R&CA Board, who believed in me and my Team.

My family, especially my Dad, my sister Heather, my uncles Chuck & Terry, and my Norma-Belle, who has believed in me and supported me in all I have done, including selling pencils!

My friends, peers and colleagues who challenge me.

John Gambaro, for all his support and words of encouragement during the toughest of times.

Chris Lucas, for believing in me, and driving me to be a better hospitality champion.

And I would like to give a special acknowledgement to Greg Hobby, whose wise counsel and encouragement throughout the writing of this book was invaluable.

# *Introduction & Testimonials*

Every crisis calls for major pivots that successful hospitality business owners must make to survive and thrive.

In this book, I'll let you in on some of the industry's key strategies to making this happen. I'll summarise decades of my own experience in hospitality to share with you the most valuable lessons I've learned.

In addition, you'll read stories of hospitality leaders who pivoted to survive and thrive. You can use their examples for inspiration and guidance to lead your hospitality business in the right direction.

By the time you finish this book, you'll know exactly what it takes to pivot through a crisis successfully.

Don't wait until it's too late to pivot! Read this book TODAY and get started to ensure your hospitality business can survive and thrive through any crisis.

*"Insightful, it's the real deal on how to succeed in one of the world's toughest businesses. "*

**Chris Lucas, CEO Lucas Group**

*"A good read for everyone in hospitality. Written by a person who cares and that's willing to go the extra mile."*

**John Gambaro, CEO Gambaro Group**

*"COVID-19 has meant that hospitality will never ever be the same. It has forced industry champions to reframe their thinking, tweak at the edges or make wholesale pivots. This book distils a lifetime of learning, couched in contagious enthusiasm. It will be the go to bible for navigating the choppy sea ahead. Wes is a leader with integrity and commercial sensitivity. In a short period of time he has left footsteps in my life and earned my trust. I am proud to call him a friend and even prouder of his ability to turn around this book. Do yourself a favour and read it immediately."*

**Salvatore Malatesta, CEO & Creative Director, ST, ALi**

*"The industry I have dedicated my life to is something I love with all I have. Over the years I have bleed with my fellow hospitality workmates and together we have helped forge the vibrant and world class restaurant scene we have had the privilege of enjoying. Our industry has always been one filled with loyal and passionate people who give all they have without wanting anything in return. We are here to serve and create memoires for all who intrust us. Now the world is under attack and our future is uncertain. Now we are the ones who are in need of service, we need guidance and leadership in managing the legal and political landscape of our uncertain future. Wes has been the light our industry has longed for and needed."*

**Shane Delia, Director Delia Group**

*"You are writing about a very complex, tough and intimidating time in global restaurant history. And in your writing, you are dis-arming the monster. You are showing the reader how to be stronger, smarter and in control. I am reminded of an ancient Samurai saying: "The devil whispered, 'You will not survive the storm.' And the warrior replied, 'I am the storm.' And you, my very dear friend, are the storm."*

**Greg Hobby, CEO Taylor & Holmes Catering**

*"An incredibly inspiring journey from young man to Hospitality savour, a "modern day champion "on a journey to save the Hospitality Industry one venue at a time. By applying the guidance and use of the 7 key principles outlined in this book you will have the best chance of success, as Wes says "survive to thrive" This book needs to sit front and centre of every person's bookcase, it needs to be your "go to" in times of need or better still read it and read it again so that when you need to draw on practical problem solving you will be ready. I couldn't stop reading the book!"*

**Venessa Barnes, Food Logic**

*#1 Wes Lambert – "The Rock Star of Aussie Hospitality".*

**Daniel Hakim, CEO of the Club of United Business (CUB)**

# CHAPTER ONE
# *Becoming a Hospitality Champion*

There's a saying, 'If you can't stand the heat, get out of the kitchen.' I'm sure you've heard that before. You may even have said it… or had it said to you.

What I have learned through both my career and life experiences, expressed in the following pages, first took root in my mind in the crucible of a restaurant kitchen.

One never knows what paths life will take, how many twists and turns are to be endured. Rarely does one know how or where the sum of those experiences will culminate. In my case, they brought me back to my beginnings. My pathway to climbing the ladder to becoming a Hospitality Champion began humbly as a 14-year-old in San Antonio, Texas, USA.

It all started with my first job in hospitality at Wendy's, a fast-food restaurant, to help my family during a very hard time. It was not glamorous or exciting flipping hamburgers, but it did instil a hospitality spirit in me that grew through many roles.

We all begin our hospitality journey somewhere for many different reasons, and we all have amazing stories to share. Little did I know that once the food was in my veins, it would be the lifeblood of my life. I wanted to, I needed to know more, do you?

This is how I first came into contact with the hospitality industry. Little did I know that it would set me on a long and exciting path to where I am right now…

## Climbing the Ladder

When I was between 14 and 15 years old, I worked hard flipping hamburgers at Wendy's during an entire summer in Texas to help my family. And in the years after my mother's passing in 1990, I got a job as a waiter in Bainbridge, Georgia, my new hometown, one my father's family has lived in as far back as the 1700s. Gradually, I started understanding how the hospitality industry worked and still, I wanted and needed more.

I continued along the hospitality path while enrolled at Emory University's Goizueta Business School in Atlanta, Georgia, working server shifts after classes at the Spaghetti Factory on Ponce de Leon, just a few kilometres from the campus. It was not easy studying and working at the same time, but a fire was burning in me to learn as much as I could about hospitality as I studied business.

Upon graduation with a BBA in Finance, I was soon employed as an investment banker at Restaurant Capital, SunTrust Bank. This was the first time I was exposed to more than operations, and began my understanding of the true nature of the hospitality business and the financial aspects of the industry. It was eye-opening, and I embraced everything I could learn about cash flow, financial reporting and other relevant financial aspects of running a hospitality business.

This wasn't the only valuable knowledge that I gained from that job. I managed a venue called Tongue & Groove at night while banking during the day, and forged strong and fruitful relationships in my network of hospitality champions, which led to me opening my first venue in 2004. Along with two partners who had observed my work in the industry, we built and opened Compound which, at the time, was the largest hospitality venue in the US – of 10,000 sqm in three buildings on 1.4 acres of land.

We sold Compound in 2006 to our largest competitor, and I moved to Thailand for an 'Eat, Pray, Love' year. But I could not get hospitality out of my veins, so I bought an Irish pub along with a new mate, Lei. I had never run a pub but was eager to learn. Within a year it was totally renovated, with operations leaned and revenue doubled, which allowed me to sell my share to my business partner for double my original investment and embark on a new hospitality journey in Australia.

**Partnering Up with Big Names**

Landing on the shores of Australia, I came with big dreams not knowing what the future would hold. Within weeks, I met Kingsley Smith, the founder of Kingsley's Restaurant Group, and whom I consider to be one of the most valuable mentors of my hospitality journey. I'll tell you this story in more detail a bit later in the book.

Like me, Kingsley had been working in hospitality since a young age. We worked together to restructure his original private company into Pacific Restaurant Group Ltd (PRG Ltd), the first full-service public restaurant

Group in Australia. We worked tirelessly to write the company prospectus, employee prospectus, to IPO and raise the much-needed funds to grow.

We spent years growing PRG Ltd and closed many successful deals. One of the most notable was with Jamie Oliver whom I met in Melbourne at a cocktail event just before one of his live cooking show events. At the time, Australia was his third-largest audience right behind the UK and Germany.

Jaime and I clicked straight away, with him introducing me to the CEO of his international restaurant expansion group and other key executives. This was the seed that allowed our partnership to grow, and after a year of due diligence and capital raising, we signed the Master Franchise for Jamie's Italian in Australia and New Zealand.

We landed a few other major successes within the PRG Ltd, which resulted in its massive growth over a 5-year period. Enough to catch the attention of other Groups leading to a trade sale at a significant increase to what was raised from our initial IPO.

## Leading the Hospitality Industry

Today, I'm the CEO of Restaurant & Catering Australia (R&CA), an industry association peak body which lobbies on behalf of the interests of the entire restaurant, catering and function centre industry in Australia. And to think that it all started with a summer job at Wendy's. Looking back, this extensive experience at all levels is what gave me invaluable knowledge and skills to help the hospitality industry thrive.

Just recently, I worked closely with many businesses to help them get through the perfect storm of drought, fires, floods, and most recently, the COVID-19 pandemic. Whether you're working in or invested in the hospitality industry or not, you know that the past few years have been challenging for hospitality professionals around the world. And it all culminated this year with the global pandemic. Like many other industries, hospitality is facing yet another huge challenge.

# *The Perfect Storm*

As far as crises go, Australia has seen it all in the past few years. And even though it is no stranger to floods, droughts and fires, it's hit some dangerous and dark records in recent times. We've faced so many challenges that had a massive impact not just on the hospitality industry, but the entire nation and the world.

For three years to mid-2019, Australia had been suffering from the biggest drought in the past 400 years. Many farmers struggled to keep food on their tables, especially in Eastern Australia. Some areas have suffered drought periods of seven years.

Paired with heatwaves and strong winds, this created conditions for the next catastrophe – a bushfire like we've never seen before.

The fire wiped out almost 16 million hectares of land across all Australian territories. Thousands of homes got destroyed, and 33 people lost their lives. According to estimates, the fire killed over a billion animals. And those are conservative estimates.

More than 11.3 million people were affected by the smoke that the fire produced, resulting in hazardous air quality that lasted for days and weeks.

As if we haven't had enough catastrophes, the start of 2020 heralded massive floods. The silver lining was that those floods extinguished around a third of fires in New South Wales. Of course, the floods also put thousands of people in danger and destroyed many properties.

But what was yet to appear may change the face of hospitality for years to come.

## The Escalation

Still reeling from blazing fires and massive floods, the coronavirus pandemic exploded into view when hospitality businesses were battered and broken from an affected summer season.

COVID-19 took the world by storm, and no country managed to prepare itself fully. While some were more affected than others, every corner of the world faced the consequences.

Millions of people were infected, and hundreds of thousands lost their lives. The pandemic put a huge dent into world economies, the results of which will be felt for years.

To stop the pandemic wreaking more havoc than it already had, governments across the world declared a lockdown. And while this was an effective way to protect us from getting infected, the hospitality industry took a massive hit with hundreds of thousands of jobs lost, thousands of businesses closed, and all looking to pick up the pieces in recovery.

## Hospitality in Times of Crisis

The coronavirus pandemic had a bigger negative effect on hospitality than any other crisis we've seen and more than most other industries. Social distancing, and other strict government measures, forced businesses to react with some of them closing, and others struggling to keep their heads above water with 'business unusual' means.

In April 2020, the Australian Bureau of Statistics surveyed 3,000 hospitality businesses. And the results paint a clear picture of how the pandemic affected the industry.

A mind-boggling 70% of businesses had to reduce staff hours. 43% either made workers redundant or placed them on unpaid leave. One in ten stopped working altogether.

Considering the immediately forced government restrictions, the above came as no surprise. Potential diners couldn't dine in restaurants or bars, nor could they travel. Even after the easing began, many social distancing measures remained.

Many businesses managed to struggle through and get back on track in this altered COVID-safe environment. But some weren't strong enough to survive. Worse yet, the pandemic may leave many long-term changes that businesses and diners must adapt to.

To say that these are challenging times for the hospitality industry would be a massive understatement. But does this mean that your business has to suffer and struggle, or worse yet, close?

No, it doesn't. You can survive, you can thrive. You decide your future.

## You Decide Your Future

All those crises over the past few years have shown us that there are so many things outside of our control. On your own, you can't do anything about crisis catastrophes like bushfires, the pandemic or even closer-to-home crises like divorce or unexpected circumstances. And because of this, you might feel paralysed.

No one wants to be helpless. And yet, this is exactly what the recent events caused millions of people to feel. As a business owner, you might think that you're at the mercy of what happens around you.

I'm here to prove otherwise.

You can't control the outside circumstances as much as you might wish to. But this doesn't mean that you can't take your business out of the uncertainty of 'business unusual' and on a path to thrive.

This might be hard to believe when you see how many businesses have closed their doors, have let staff go, or had to dramatically alter their lives with debt, especially in hospitality.

But believe me when I say that there's always something that you can do to rise above the chaos. There must be an action that you can take to survive and thrive – you just need to know where to look.

Every business owner knows the importance of embracing change and adapting to it. Well, now's the time to put that knowledge to the test. You must take a bold action that will help you ride out this wave of crises.

And the best part is, you don't have to do it on your own.

# *What You Will Discover in This Book*

Essentially, this book is a guide for successfully pivoting during and after a crisis. I'll show you some of the critical steps to surviving the tough periods and thriving in the good ones. You'll see the 7 Pillars of a successful hospitality business pivot, and how to apply them to your business.

I'll summarise decades of experience in this industry and share the most valuable lessons that every business owner needs. By the end of the book, you'll know what it takes to go through crises, forge a new path and come out stronger.

It's worth mentioning that I'm not just talking about national or international crises like natural disasters and pandemics. On a smaller scale, a crisis for your business may be a divorce, pressure from the competition, internal investor struggles, or anything that threatens your success.

I want you to see a crisis not as an obstacle, but a challenge. This book will help you get into the right mindset and show you what action you need to take if you want your business to achieve outstanding success.

On the pathway you have chosen, every crisis calls for a pivot. And if you don't do it, you risk going out of business. This is true regardless of your business' size. The 7 Pillars that you'll discover here are universally applicable and can support any hospitality business on its path to greatness.

CHAPTER TWO

# *Introducing the 7 Pillars of a Successful Pivot*

At the height of the COVID-19 lockdown, the Accommodation and Food Services (hospitality) industry lost 441,400 jobs according to the Australian Bureau of Statistics, representing over 30% of the total jobs in those segments of the industry. According to a survey conducted by The Monday Group, which surveyed over 200 hospitality business owners and senior executives, 9 in 10 businesses reported having to reduce headcount and salaries. And according to an IBISWorld report, the restaurant industry was expected to shrink over 25%.

Business owners are anxiously waiting for things to get back to normal. However, it may take a long time before we're back to something that resembles life before the pandemic. While life may begin to return to some normality and some businesses will recover quickly, it could take up to two years for the hospitality industry to recover.

What's more, this is just an estimate based on how things are unfolding. It's likely we'll have to face longer headwinds in hospitality as economies take time to recover locally and globally.

This assumes we don't face a second wave of the pandemic in months or years, which is a possibility. Even if a second wave does not come, some experts say that it might take years for the economy and unemployment to return to pre-COVID-19 levels. As Sarah Hunter, chief economist at BIS Oxford Economics, explained:

*'It's not just the question of the restrictions being relaxed and things snapping back to normal. That's not likely to happen. Some people's jobs won't return to normal. Their income level won't return to normal, and so they won't be spending the same way.'*

Another recent Australian Bureau of Statistics report noted only 61% of patrons were comfortable to return to restaurants and cafes, more than 3 in 4 were uncomfortable returning to large event venues, and 63% were uncomfortable flying.

Through the pandemic crisis, we saw a rise in delivery and takeaway dining, as people were forced to eat at home during lockdowns and restrictions. And, as fewer venues and suppliers reopen, and social distancing remains in place at any level reducing the number of available seats in venues (supply & demand), the price of food and drinks is likely to rise.

All of these changes will shape the recovery and the future of hospitality. You might wonder if your business will be able to survive until things are back on track.

The good news is – yes, you most certainly cannot only survive, but thrive through this crisis and any you face in the future! The key to starting down the pathway through recovery is the 7 Pillars to Pivoting through a crisis.

# *What Are the 7 Pillars to Pivoting?*

As you read in Chapter One, I built my career in hospitality from the ground up from humble beginnings in many areas of hospitality. This allowed me to gain insights and perspective from many angles and across many business types. It gave me a deep understanding of what makes each hospitality business unique and how to help make your business successful in the long run, through ups and downs.

You have made it this far, so you are also a Hospitality Champion, but if you are struggling or uncertain, I am here to help you survive and thrive through a crisis. Your journey must start with these 7 Pillars:

1. Find a Trusted Mentor
2. Understand Your Financials
3. Create a Forecast to Predict the Future
4. Make a Plan (and Measure Against it)
5. Create New Streams of Revenue
6. Execute Your Plan
7. Continue to Pivot and Make Changes as Necessary

Just by looking at the list, can you recognise some of the things that you're already doing? If so, that's great news, you are ahead of the pack! It means that you're already working towards a secure and more prosperous future for your hospitality business.

In my experience, however, many businesses don't have all of the above boxes checked. And some businesses haven't made any plans at all! This can be very dangerous as you navigate your business through a crisis. You'll read about 'not being a propeller' later and you'll understand!

Focusing on these 7 Pillars for Pivoting through a crisis allows you to make your business more immune to crises, which will inevitably come in any business life cycle. It de-risks your business and helps you get through the tough periods much more smoothly, and with more certainty for the future.

So, what does it take to make this happen?

The rest of this book will focus on each of the 7 Pillars and give an in-depth explanation of how it works. Hopefully, you'll be able to find the holes in your business and fill them to build a strong foundation to survive and thrive.

# CHAPTER THREE

# *Pillar #1 – Find a Trusted Mentor*

Soon after selling my share of the Irish Pub in Thailand in 2007, I ventured to Australia and met restaurateur Kingsley Smith. I was optimistic, encouraged by recent hospitality experiences and seeking new opportunities. Meeting and working with Kingsley turned out to be one of the most impactful opportunities that I could ever hope for!

Kingsley has always been very passionate about food and beverages, sourcing, quality and customer service, and most of all, relationships. Since meeting him over a decade ago, he has been a massive influence on my hospitality career. Today, I'm proud to call him one of my most important mentors.

I began working with Kingsley as Director of Business Development at Kingsley's Restaurant Group, the Group he founded in Sydney, that had already expanded to Brisbane and Canberra. My goal was to use my previous hospitality experience to help the company grow. For nine months, I worked tirelessly alongside Kingsley to restructure the business into a vehicle for future growth. This is how Pacific Restaurant Group Ltd (PRG Ltd) was formed.

I've learned so much from Kingsley, and his contribution to my development was invaluable. One of the main lessons he taught me was the value of relationships and how to be more human. I am naturally a 'numbers guy', but Kingsley saw I needed development and taught me how to network more effectively and provide better and more personal customer service. To this day, I haven't forgotten many of the key foundation principles Kingsley instilled in me every single day we worked together.

Together, we pitched the idea for PRG Ltd to hundreds of potential investors during an IPO on a roadshow around the country. Eventually, after many lunch meetings, dinner meetings and negotiations, we enlisted a group of shareholders and formed the strategic public company Board, which helped the business achieve massive success and a future trade sale.

Another influential figure in my life is Con Castrisos OAM. He is a well-known solicitor and restaurateur from Brisbane, and a key long-serving Board Member of Restaurant & Catering Australia (R&CA), who's mentored me tremendously in my current role. He helped me find my feet and take on the role of the CEO at R&CA with valuable negotiations advice and words of wisdom.

Con has guided my path as a lobbyist and ensured that I factored in all possible outcomes of my actions. He helped me hone my skills in dealing with the government on local, state and federal levels; his impact on my lobbying style cannot be understated.

While Kingsley and Con have been key to my becoming a Hospitality Champion, I've had many mentors throughout my career. From captains of industry to government officials, many influential leaders have guided my pathway to success.

I've also been sure to pass on the many lessons I have learned throughout my career. I've mentored many future leaders, from MBA students studying at Goizueta Business School in their business pathway, to executives from various private and publicly listed American, Asian, and Australian companies.

Why is mentoring so important?

Because there are very few things as important as learning from other's triumphs and failures. And in this chapter, I'll prove to you why mentoring is so important, and how you can find the right mentor.

# *You Don't Know What You Don't Know*

Too many business owners believe that they can do it all on their own. After working long and hard in their business, they believe no one knows their business better than they do.

Only this isn't always true, especially during and after a crisis.

When business conditions are out of your control and you hit a rough patch, you need to know how to ask for help. You must find a reputable source of actionable information that will help you push through. Otherwise, you might be heading in the wrong direction without even knowing why.

Even though I have been working in hospitality for decades, I continue to have many people whom I look up to. I believe that there's always someone who can teach you valuable lessons that you'll use to survive and thrive.

Have you found this person so far? If not, it's time to start looking!

A mentor can be anyone who holds the information that you need. It doesn't even have to be someone from your industry. It could be a trusted friend, lawyer, accountant, or someone from your business club. A mentor can also be a business leader in any sector, or even your competitor. As long as someone can help you to look at things from a fresh perspective and teach you something, they're an ideal mentor.

If you're still not convinced why it's critical to have mentors, let me attempt to change your mind.

# 5 Reasons Why a Mentor Is Critical to Success

There is nothing wrong with following your instincts or knowledge, you are a hospitality professional. But in many cases, this won't be enough when conditions get tough. The last thing you want to do is to stubbornly get stuck in your own head and keep doing business the same way for too long. In an industry that changes as rapidly as hospitality, this can be very dangerous.

So here are five reasons why a mentor is critical to success:

## 1. They Have the Knowledge that You Can't Get Elsewhere

Where do you gather the knowledge and skills that you need to build a successful business? If you're like most business owners, the answer would likely be online, through webinars, books and conventions, and even by watching the competitors.

But here's the thing:

A mentor can give you the kind of knowledge that no other source can provide. They can give you *real-life experiences*. This is one of the most valuable assets that you can get for free.

There are massive gaps between theoretical knowledge and *real-life* business practice. Success in the hospitality industry, or any industry for that matter, is never a straight line. The path to success is a complex web of directions; a mentor helps you gain the clarity that you need to ensure you choose the right one.

Mentors can help you avoid costly mistakes and experiments that rob you of time and energy. Why try to figure out something on your own when there's someone who's been there and can show you a better way?

## 2. A Mentor Helps You Develop Emotional Intelligence

Along with experience, mentors often have the maturity that every business owner needs. Even if you believe that you're in full control over your emotions, this might not always be true.

Imagine being a business that had to close down temporarily during the bushfires, floods or COVID-19. In all likelihood, for many of you, that may well have been the case.

If so, how did you feel?

'Helpless, paralysed, and afraid' is only one of the possible answers. But believe it or not, there are many business owners who didn't let these crises, or any before, scare them. And you can learn a lot from such people.

Having a firm grasp on your emotions is vital to weathering the storms that you'll face. And a mentor can provide calming advice to send fear packing.

### 3. Your Business Can Live Longer

This is possibly one of the most important reasons why you should find a mentor when you start a business, or as soon as you experience any crisis or see one coming. After all, you want your business to survive and thrive while you pivot. Then you want to make sure that you keep growing once the tough times pass so you are stronger for the next crisis.

A mentor can help make sure that your business lives longer. This isn't just my opinion based on experience – it's a well-researched fact.

According to recent research, 30% of new businesses don't make it past the first 24 months, especially in a crisis. What's more, *half* of all businesses will disappear in the first five years.

A survey from the UPS Store showed that 70% of businesses whose owners are under mentorship survive for five or more years. That's double the rate of those businesses whose owners don't get mentored!

The same survey showed that 88% of business owners believe that having a mentor has been invaluable to their success.

### 4. A Mentor Keeps You on the Right Path

The 'shiny object syndrome' is present way too often, even with the most focused entrepreneurs. The hospitality industry is no exception. Not having a sharp focus on your goals can lead you off the path to success, and even threaten your chances of survival.

My grandfather, Charles Wesley Markham, always used to tell me:

*'Wes, you need to keep your eye on the prize.'*

He started his career working at one of the first Frito Lay plants in Dallas, Texas. By the end of his almost 36-year career, he had been the General Manager of almost every Frito Lay manufacturing plant in America and ended up an executive in the Headquarters in Dallas.

Needless to say, my grandfather was one of my biggest inspirations and mentors. He taught me to keep my focus, which is something that every business owner should have.

And this is exactly what mentors can do for you. They can be guides that will make sure you don't steer off course. They can help you build focus on good habits, long-term goals and work ethic that will take you to where you want to be.

## 5. A Mentor Opens Up Networking Opportunities

Ask hospitality leaders about their key factors of success, and virtually all of them will mention the same thing – connections.

No one in business can make it on their own, no one is an island, at least not in the long run. Because of this, it is vital to surround yourself with energetic go-getters and people who take action, not just talk about taking action. Make no mistake, your successful competitors are certainly doing this.

Mentors help you unlock endless networking opportunities. They can introduce you to other business people who can have a massive impact on their and your success. Trust me, you do not want to miss out on an opportunity to connect with business leaders.

With time, you can form many fruitful relationships that can take your business to the next level. Open yourself up to them, and your chances of success will skyrocket.

These are just a few of the key reasons why having a mentor can make a world of difference to your business. But what traits make an ideal mentor?

# *The Traits of a Great Mentor*

As you go about pivoting and growing your business, especially through a crisis, you'll encounter numerous people with even more opinions. Just because you are given many opinions, it doesn't necessarily mean that you should take all of them as sound, solid business advice that pertains to your unique situation.

While mentors can come from all walks of life, not everyone who has advice for you can be a mentor. In fact, there are **10 key traits** you should look out for if you're going to trust them as an influential figure in your business.

## 1. They Have Your Best Interest in Mind

As I mentioned, many people may tell you how to do your job as a business owner. They'll suggest all sorts of 'off-path' ideas that you might just end up considering. However, you will survive and thrive if you are able to weed out the advice that doesn't help you pivot and grow.

And the best way to do this is by confirming if someone has your best interest in mind.

When someone presents their advice and themselves as a potential mentor, examine your relationship with them. Do they truly care if you succeed or fail? More importantly, *why* do they care?

You should strive to only turn to the people who genuinely want to see you succeed. Otherwise, they might unintentionally harm your business and wrap it up as a piece of advice that you should take. So, before you consider someone's advice or mentorship, think about whether they truly care if you succeed.

## 2. They Have No Stake in the Decision

Finding a mentor who won't be impacted by your decisions is always the safest bet. Why is it so important to get someone objective on board?

Because it's hard to know if there's a hidden agenda behind an individual's advice, even if it's unintentional. While it's ideal to find an external mentor with your best interest in mind, you will probably quickly find that many internal stakeholders will offer well-meaning advice.

If you're not 100% sure that your ideal mentors have something at stake in your decisions, keep searching for those that don't have any skin in the game and can give you an objective, outside perspective.

## 3. They're Able to Offer Outside Perspective

Ideal mentors could be someone outside of your business or industry. And there's a lot of value in finding such people and asking for their mentorship.

While the hospitality industry is unique and complicated, it's complexity is not isolated. You can find many mentors from other industries who can make a massive impact on your success as they can provide outside-the-box insight that you might not have gained.

There's a wealth of business knowledge outside of hospitality that can make a significant difference to your success. If you always stay in your lane, you may not be able to find that knowledge.

So, don't discredit or reject mentors just because they don't have the same background as you. Embrace those that can share different perspectives, and you can open yourself up to many profitable ideas to thrive and survive.

## 4. They Give Real Advice (and Straight Talk)

In this social media and instant information age, everyone can claim to be an expert on just about anything. They land a few successes and position themselves as an authority. But just because they see themselves this way doesn't mean that you always should as well.

A good mentor won't give you any vague, watered-down advice or a pep talk. They'll hit the nail right on the head and offer you actionable information, even if it's not what you want to hear.

Luckily, it's easy to distinguish a real mentor from someone who just claims to be one. All you have to do is ask yourself if you can truly apply their advice in a concrete manner to your particular business.

Can they give you clear and concise directions that you can follow? Is there any evidence that their methods truly work?

While there are many trustworthy people out there, you shouldn't believe everything that you hear. Find proof in their actions over many years and in many business situations to show you that the mentorship can truly push your business forward, and only then consider them to be a mentor.

You need a mentor who will be honest with you and tell what you need to hear, regardless of whether you like it or not. The last thing you need is a cheerleader that will agree with everything that you say unconditionally and not challenge your assumptions. This undermines the whole purpose of having a mentor.

Find a mentor who won't hesitate to tell you if you're wrong. And when they suggest to you what to do, ingest it, take it to heart, listen and don't shoot down ideas. You will thank them in the long run for their honesty.

## 5. They're a Leader

A leader's mindset is something that you can't put a price on. Even if they lose everything, a true leader can find their way back because their minds are wired to be driven to succeed. Someone with a leader's mindset doesn't let obstacles and challenges overcome them. Instead, they know that there's always a solution and a way forward.

And this is exactly the kind of person that you need to pivot and grow through a crisis.

There are many business owners who didn't back away from the fight in front of the pandemic, bushfires, or other crises that threatened to affect their businesses. Rather, they saw the challenge as another change that they need to address and adapt to.

In fact, many leaders ultimately embraced the crises as an opportunity to pivot and bring important changes to their business.

Is this how you saw the perfect storm that the hospitality industry has been facing in the past few years? If not, you can definitely benefit from the guidance of a mentor who did.

Many crises that happen are outside of your control. The only thing that you can influence is how you'll react to them. You get to choose how you'll respond and pivot, and this is what makes or breaks your business, not the crisis itself.

A mentor can help you get into this mindset and see any crises from a different point of view. And when your mindset changes, your business will as well.

## 6. They Have Experience

It is incredibly important to distinguish true mentors from those who try to convince you that they are. In most cases, the main difference will be in their level of experience.

In both business and life, there is hardly anything as valuable as experience. It's what makes you evolve and grow without limits.

But there's something crucial that you need to know about experience. It is not something that you measure with time. Instead, it's something that is measured by the lessons learned, both in success and failure.

A potential mentor might claim that they have 20 years of experience. When, in fact, what they really have is one year of experience 20 times. If they have a track record of doing the same things over and over, their experience isn't as valuable.

This is why, when seeking a mentor, you shouldn't focus on how long they've been in the game. Rather, focus on what they've filled that time with, and ask about failures as well as triumphs.

Valuable experience includes knowledge, struggle, and trial and error. It involves many mistakes that taught lessons on how to do business better next time.

## 7. They Have Failures on Their Record

Failure is such a scary word. In fact, it's what most people in businesses dread.

It means that you messed something up or made a mistake that may have negatively affected your business due to that poor decision.

If this is how you see failure, you need to change your perspective now! Ironically, it's this kind of mindset that makes people and businesses fail in the first place.

If you knew how valuable failure was, you'd never fear it again. If anything, you'd embrace it like a true ideal mentor, or like a leader does.

Many business owners might not yet see it this way. When you fail, your ego gets bruised. The consequences of that failure discourage you. You become afraid to take further action because you don't want it to happen again.

All of this is nothing but a product of fear and wrong mindset.

What really happens when you fail is that you learn. You see that your decision didn't work, you are given the opportunity to learn from your mistake, which shows you what not to do in your objective to get it right next time.

There is no one perfect way to become successful in hospitality that applies to everyone. If there was, it would be in a book every entrepreneur would read to become an industry giant overnight.

Instead, you need to figure out what works for your unique position, which involves taking all sorts of action. Many of those actions will be wrong, and there's nothing wrong with that! If you learn from that failure, it is a stepping-stone to success.

Good mentors are not afraid to talk about their failures. They own those failures and can share that knowledge with you openly.

Beware of mentors who tell you incredible success stories without showing you what it really took to get there. Learn from those who will teach you that failure is a necessary part of the pathway to success. When this becomes your default mindset, you'll be unstoppable.

## 8. They're a Well-Rounded Businessperson

When you choose a mentor, you want it to be someone that you respect and look up to. It needs to be a person who you aspire to become in one way or another. They should have something that you need and are willing to teach you.

In other words, you need a well-rounded person who excels at whatever business they are in.

But what does it mean to be a well-rounded businessperson? There are a few characteristics that you should look out for:

- **Confidence** – A mentor should have the kind of healthy confidence that doesn't cross over to arrogance or egotism.
- **Discipline and time management** – Do you know those people who just seem to be on top of everything at all times? This is how an ideal mentor should seem.

- **A can-do attitude** – Well-rounded businesspeople don't have the word *'can't'* in their vocabulary. They always find a way around crises or challenges.
- **Continuous improvement** – People who think they know it all become complacent and stop learning. A mentor should inspire you to keep bettering yourself at all times.
- **Consistency** – Consistency without rigidness is an invaluable trait. Good mentors know when to follow the rules, and when to allow room for flexibility and change.

These are some of the key traits that you should look for in a businessperson that you want to learn from. So, think hard whether there's anyone in your environment that meets the criteria. If so, they could be a potential mentor.

## 9. They Have Operational Ability

You don't need to find one ideal mentor who has all the knowledge you require to pivot your business. In fact, finding one person that meets all the criteria would be challenging at best. You should actively seek experts in their fields and get them on board.

For example, you might have an outstanding accountant who goes far beyond crunching the numbers. They have a deep understanding of your financials and can provide invaluable insight. On the other hand, they might have no idea about hospitality operations.

In this case, you should work with that accountant and look to other potential mentors who possess operational expertise and understand your process challenges to maximise their profitability.

Even if operations is their primary skill set, you should still consider them as a mentor. Keen operational skills are of utmost importance in a pivot. They can help you see inefficiencies and holes in your business, where you need to pivot, and where the pitfalls may occur.

## 10. They're Inquisitive and Approachable

A good mentor will always keep you on your toes. They understand that what worked yesterday won't necessarily yield results today or tomorrow. Every potential mentor worth their salt will speak of the importance of continuous improvement. They should make sure that you do as well. And if you need advice they don't have an answer for, an ideal mentor will go out of their way to help you find it.

This means that they should be available to you at critical times. While they can't hand-hold or do your job for you, you should be able to rely on them for guidance during tough times.

It's always a good idea to set up a schedule and meet with your mentor regularly. This will give you both the structure that you can follow to discuss all important topics during and after pivots as well as changes to your business. And you should meet them even more regularly when your business is in crisis.

## *Find the Guidance You Need*

Hopefully, you now better understand why having an ideal mentor is so important. I would not be a Hospitality Champion if it wasn't for the guidance of influential people showing me the way and continuing to help guide my path. Finding good mentors is the key foundation pillar to help pivot your business through the crisis.

Now that you know what to look for in mentors, think about the businesspeople and advisors in your life. As I explained, it is not critical for one person to hold all the advice you may need. You should surround yourself with multiple, well-qualified mentors if you want to push through hardship and come out on top.

With that said, there's one important thing that you need to keep in mind:

A mentor is not a cure-all, and they're not someone who'll take your business and pivot it for you. At the end of the day, you're responsible for deciding the right pivots for your business. You need to hold yourself accountable for your actions rather than expect someone to hand the solution to you.

Remember that good mentors provide guidance and may help you unlock opportunities that you might not see. What you do with that information and skills is ultimately up to you, don't expect mentors will magically solve all your problems. It comes down to learning to stand on your own two feet and leading your business through challenges.

While finding a mentor will make things much easier, there's still a lot that you have to do if you want to crisis-proof your business. In the next chapter, I'll show you something that you must focus on as soon as possible if you want your business to survive and thrive in the long run.

CHAPTER FOUR

# Pillar #2 – Understand Your Financials

An unexpected crisis can wreak havoc on hospitality businesses. Almost overnight, some restaurants experienced a revenue downturn of up to 50%. This is exactly what happened to Emily Raven's popular café, My Kingdom for a Horse, in Adelaide. The first Sunday after the health restrictions, Raven saw a downturn of 25%. The very next day, it reached 50%.

Immediately, there was uncertainty and confusion. In her own words:

*'Do we keep taking bookings? Do we keep serving people knowing there's a risk? It costs $18,000 a week to keep a business of mine, just to exist, so any closure has to be carefully orchestrated.'*

Raven is just one of the many hospitality business owners who faced serious challenges during the crisis. George Kasimatis, the owner of George's, also in Adelaide, said,

*'We have had massive cancellations, especially with group corporate and social bookings moving forward.'*

A similar downturn affected Janie Kammer's Karma and Crow in Richmond. Kammer said that numbers were dropping every day and that she'd never seen such a decline before.

These are just a few examples of the tens of thousands of hospitality venues that were dramatically affected by the pandemic crisis. And let's not forget about caterers around the country, who experienced an 80-100% cancel rate as function centres closed.

Tens of thousands of hospitality businesses in Australia took a serious financial hit and it will take time and much effort to recover. And yours was likely one of them, as were the millions of hospitality businesses across the globe faced with massive drops in revenue.

Still, most hospitality business owners are hopeful about the future, trying to figure out a path to get back on track. A KPMG survey of 225 mid-market businesses revealed that 79% felt 'confident' in their ability to recover from the COVID-19 crisis. If you're among them, the next pillar after obtaining solid advice from ideal mentors is getting a firm grasp on, and understanding of, your financials.

Otherwise, how can you know which changes you need to make? If you don't have a clear picture of your financial standing, it's nearly impossible to make smart and profitable decisions.

This chapter will discuss why every hospitality business owner needs to know their numbers so they can recover their business and thrive.

# *The Numbers Don't Lie*

Many hospitality business owners are reluctant to do their financials. Those who do may struggle to keep them up-to-date and find it challenging to track all the key numbers, key performance indicators and ratios.

Rather, they often wait until the end of the year and hear good or bad news from their accountant or bookkeeper. You may have a fantastic accountant, or an entire team for that matter, but it is critical that you know your numbers.

Numbers are the most accurate representation of your business' health. There is no better information that can reveal a clearer picture of your standing than precise numbers. You are responsible for knowing your financial position.

While your accountant can crunch the numbers and give you the insight that you need, they're not responsible for pivoting your business through or after a crisis. Take control of your business' future by starting with what it takes to 'turn on the aircon', your business' break-even point.

# *What Is Your Break-Even Point?*

Before a crisis, your business revenue may have been growing or stable, and you may have been profitable or losing money. As you pivot, one of the key indicators you need to know is your break-even point, the magic number when you have covered all your fixed and variable costs and can start making a profit.

There are too many hospitality owners to count that have no idea about their break-even point. And many that do, rely on their bookkeeper or accountant to calculate the number, often after it's too late.

When you know this number, you'll possess the most critical information about your business. This includes:

- Your menu and associated profitability
- How big of a downturn you can face before you start seeing losses
- How many units of your product you must sell to be profitable
- What impact would discounts and price cuts have on your profitability
- How much you need to raise your prices in order to compensate for rising fixed costs

Knowing this single number is one of the most important lessons many business owners learn too late, but knowing it will keep you ahead of the competition as you pivot.

But how do you calculate it?

There are actually a few ways to do it. A simple first step is using one of the most basic formulas.

The formula relies on your Gross Profit (revenue minus cost of goods sold) and Fixed Costs (including Labour in this example) to work out your break-even point:

$$\textit{Break-even point = Fixed Costs / Gross Profit.}$$

So, if your total fixed costs is $50,000, and your Gross Profit margin is 60%, you'd need $83,333 in revenue to break-even.

But how much do you need to sell in order to get there?

To calculate this, you need to work out your contribution margin:

*Contribution margin = sales price – variable costs (all costs of making the item)*

You may have dozens of amazing choices on your menu and an otherwise diversified range of offers. But to keep things simple, let's assume that an item menu price is $50 and that variable costs of that item are $15. In this case, your contribution margin is $35.

To get your break-even point, use the following formula:

*Break-even point = fixed costs / contribution margin*

In our example, this would be:

*$50,000 / $35 = 1,429*

You'd have to sell 1,429 of that menu item to break-even. Of course, every menu item you offer will yield different contribution margins, so you need to calculate the break-even point for each of them. A bit later in this chapter, I'll show you another reason why knowing your contribution margin is critical, and teach you a concept that can work wonders for your profitability.

But for now, you can see that figuring out your break-even point is not as daunting when you calculate it by menu item. Knowing this number is absolutely critical to navigate your business through a crisis and thrive, but it's far from the only key indicator that you should know. Are you familiar with revenue calculation? What about fixed and variable costs? Do you know your COGS (Costs of Goods Sold), or Prime Cost (COGS + Labour) or EBITDA (Earnings before Interest, Taxes, Depreciation, and Amortization)?

If not, you've got some work to do to fully understand your finances. Finances aren't the most exciting part of your business, but it's vital to know them backwards and forwards. The sooner you do, the quicker you can get through tough times with confidence.

Let's dive a bit deeper into these numbers!

# Create Regular Profit and Loss (P&L) Statements

Even before a crisis strikes, a regular P&L statement puts all the critical numbers at your fingertips. You should complete them monthly and aim to have them done by you, or your bookkeeper/accountant, in the first week or two of the month, so you can review them and make changes quickly when/where you see problems!

If you are completing your P&Ls yourself, here are the steps that you need to take:

**1. Calculate Your Revenue**

The first thing you need to do is calculate all the sales revenue that you received in the previous period. If you run a P&L monthly, you must include all your revenue from the previous month, regardless of whether you've collected it or not.

Most hospitality businesses are cash businesses, so we will assume customers pay when served, but you may be a caterer with accounts receivable from customers for past events. So, factor in your accounts receivable and cash/credit card sales. Make sure that you encompass all your revenue, wherever it came from or however small it is from your POS.

**2. Calculate Your COGS & Labour**

Your Cost of Goods Sold (COGS) & Labour play vital roles in your profitability. No matter what's on your menu, you must know exactly how much it costs to make and serve.

COGS encompasses every expense related to your supplies and ingredients. This includes everything from food and drinks to condiments and garnishes. Know exactly what your COGS is so that you avoid overspending and having cost blowouts affecting your profit.

Labour is your payroll and ALL the associated costs of payroll, like payroll tax, leave entitlements and superannuation.

Adding your COGS and Labour together will give you your Prime Costs, an extremely important number for your business discussed further below.

## 3. Calculate Operating Expenses

Other than COGS and Labour, you must factor in your operating expenses to determine your profitability. This includes things like rent & outgoings, insurance, telephone/internet, cleaning, utilities; all the expenses you incur to run your business day-to-day.

When you have all your invoices, operating expenses calculated, subtract them from Gross Profit, and what's left is your Operating Profit.

## 4. Add Your Additional Income

If there are any additional sources of revenue that you haven't factored in, this is where you should do it. Typically, this will include things like dividends from investments or interest income. Hospitality businesses do not typically receive this income, but some may, so it's been included.

This is how you'll get your EBITDA (Earnings before Interest, Taxes, Depreciation and Amortization).

## 5. Calculate Taxes, Interest, Depreciation, and Amortization

You may have Taxes due or Interest Payments, and any business with Assets will have some non-cash Depreciation expenses of writing those Assets off each month/year and a few may have Amortization expenses related to Intangible expenses.

Once you have those numbers calculated, subtract them all from your EBITDA, and you'll get your Net Profit/Loss.

You will also need good P&Ls at tax time. Tax preparation can be a tedious and stressful process. Many business owners always feel like there's something that they might be missing. But the only reason why this happens is that they don't update their P&L statements regularly.

If you do it all last-minute, it's almost impossible to avoid stress and confusion. But if you keep your statements neat and have all the information sorted out, you'll be ready for tax season. And this will save you a lot of headaches.

The process can be straightforward but may take you some months to master. Again, many of you will rely on your bookkeeper or accountant to create your P&Ls but it is critically important to understand the parts of your P&Ls as indicators of your financial standing.

## Understanding Trends

Most P&Ls today will be generated in QuickBooks, MYOB or Xero. Once you have a good grasp of your P&Ls, it's equally important to understand the trends of your hospitality business.

One of the main reasons to calculate regular monthly P&L statements is to identify trends. Trends show how your business behaves throughout the year, allowing you to notice the patterns that can help you make smarter decisions. Trends may include periods of higher or lower revenue, or increases (or decreases) in your COGS, Labour or Operating Expenses that may need your attention to reign in to improve profit.

When you hit any crisis, your revenue may be affected, and profits will be at risk. By knowing the trends of your business, you will understand where you need to pivot first!

When you face challenges like the COVID-19 pandemic or bushfires, increasing sales is not an option. In fact, loss of revenue, most likely, is the crisis in your business. You'll immediately know that it's time to look at your COGS, Labour and Operating Expenses and make firm plans to bring them down in line with the drop in revenue.

This is just one simple example of how P&L statements help you to determine the right action to take at the start of any crisis. When you know all your important numbers, you'll have much more control of the direction in which your business goes as you plan your pivots!

## Prime Costs are KEY

Prime Costs (also known as Direct Costs) are the most important key performance indicators of your hospitality business. Prime Costs, as noted above, are the sum of your COGS and Labour costs. Your Prime Costs are the costs you incur to make and serve the food and beverage in your hospitality business and should be used to help you manage your revenue and spending to ensure you make a profit!

$$Prime\ Costs = COGS + Labour\ Costs$$

Generally, all food and beverage costs and all staff costs are Prime Costs and do not include Operating Expenses like rent, insurance, or utilities.

Why are Prime Costs key to your business, especially in a crisis?

Prime Costs make up the largest costs of your business, so must be closely managed. Prime Costs are variable and cannot be budgeted for as easily as fixed costs like rent or insurance rates. Suppliers can change their wholesale prices month on month, and it may be harder to pass those costs on when they vary month on month by changing menu prices. And seasonality, or even dramatic drops in revenue caused by a crisis, can affect your staffing, rosters and Labour costs.

But, if you monitor your Prime Costs closely, and are agile, and pivot when needed, you **CAN** control them! You control which suppliers you use in your business and your roster. Keeping an eye on your Prime Costs will help you to more effectively price your menus, manage your order inventory, manage your roster and establish short-term sales goals and promotions.

## Prime Cost Ratios

Now that you understand how important Prime Costs are, you also need to understand Prime Cost Ratios and reasons why they may be off and affecting your business

Once you have calculated Prime Costs as COGS + Labour, you want to calculate your Prime Cost %.

*Prime Cost / Total Sales Revenue x 100 = Prime Cost %*

And now you'll likely be wondering what a good Prime Cost % is. It varies wildly per jurisdiction, but in Australia, a Prime Cost % between 60-70% of revenue is a standard range. It will depend mainly on your food type COGS as Labour rates are standard across the industry.

Above 70%, and you may find it very difficult to cover your Operating Expense and still make a profit, and this is especially true both during and after a crisis as you pivot back to profitability.

## Forecasting Expenses

As your business hits a crisis of any kind, you need to quickly assess your Operating Expenses and where you can make immediate cuts and changes. Having a regularly updated P&L at hand will make decision making and immediate planning much easier to manage as you can see what your largest expenses historically have been.

Otherwise, you might lose control over the fixed costs of your business and pour a lot of money down the drain without seeking relief as you react to and pivot through the crisis.

## Making Plans for the Future

Another key reason to create regular P&Ls and begin to understand your financial position is when a crisis hits and you need to make significant changes to your business quickly.

How can you know what impact those changes will have? In many cases, those business owners who don't know their numbers make a lot of assumptions and guesstimates. And that's no way to pivot your business through a crisis.

When you are faced with adversity and must make operational changes to your business, you must know exactly how they will affect your finances. You can rarely predict things with 100% accuracy. But it's better to have a plan and forecast than go in almost completely blind.

I'll expand more on this in the next chapter where I'll discuss forecasting in greater detail. But for now, it is important to understand that you can't predict the future without understanding the past and the present. And just about all the data that you need is in your P&L statements.

Of course, the above examples are just the tip of the iceberg of all the reasons why you need to create your P&L statements regularly. But I hope that they're convincing enough to get you to actually do it. So much power can be found in your numbers, so make sure that you leverage it. Numbers don't lie.

But if that's not enough, here's another *very* good reason for working out your numbers.

# Penny Profit vs. Cost

I promised earlier I'd tell you why you must know your contribution margin. So, here is an example that was published in the Restaurant & Catering Magazine in 2011.

Financial Controller at Pacific Restaurant Group Ltd devised what I, at the time, called the Moët test. At one of our most profitable restaurants, Chophouse Steakhouse in Sydney, we listed Moët et Chandon champagne for $99 per bottle. At the time, and even now, it sounds crazy, right? After all, most of our competitors had it listed for $130-$140 at the time. So why would I sell it so much below the going rate?

Because we were able to secure a wholesale price of $35 per bottle in volume, which means that my contribution margin was $64. So, here's where the magic kicks in:

By selling Moët et Chandon at such a reasonable price, customers noticed we were offering a luxury menu item at massive value. And because of that, they'd normally buy two bottles instead of one!

As a result, I'd make $130 instead of the typical margin on one bottle. And as you may know, there are very few wines on wine lists with that level contribution, not in most hospitality venues! And customers were ecstatic at the experience, returning again and again.

The results of the test were fantastic and led to spreadsheets that the managers updated each month with the contribution margin of not only Moët et Chandon but all the menu items, giving us critical per-menu-item knowledge. Chophouse was a Star of the Group and achieved a handful of months where they'd come close to a 40% store EBITDA.

That is fundamentally what Penny Profit vs. Cost is all about. You can't spend percentages. Instead, it all comes down to how many items you can sell that have a higher contribution margin!

Have you ever tried taking this approach and focusing on the value that your customers receive to drive revenue? You certainly will need to as you pivot through a crisis, and if not, here's one more thing that you'll want to try:

# *Menu Engineering*

What does your menu look like? If you're like most businesses, you might list all your white wines, and then all your red wines, by varietal. You might also sort the menu in descending order by price listing your entrees, mains, desserts or nibbles from lowest to highest price.

This is what the majority of restaurateurs do. But it doesn't exactly lead to the behaviour that you want from your customers and certainly does not lead to the increased contribution margin noted above. Why not put the items with the highest contribution margin in the middle. And then those items with the lowest contribution at the top, and the premium ones at the bottom of your menu.

But why does it make sense to do this?

**Leveraging Human Nature**

It makes sense for the premium items to be at the bottom of your menu. They're usually for well-off customers or for special events, so there's not as much attention there.

But do you know why your items with the highest margin contribution should go in the middle?

It's because people will likely choose them out of habit or standard learned behaviour. You see, diners are often hard-wired to choose from the middle of the menu. For example, businesspeople won't go for the more expensive wines because their company wouldn't allow them to and they have seen their co-workers, peers or boss do the same. But at the same time, they don't want to look cheap and choose the cheapest ones.

I have heard hundreds, maybe even thousands of stories from business diners who won't buy the cheapest, or the most expensive, but pick items from the middle of the menu. A recent New York Times article noted: 'research shows that diners tend to order neither the most nor least expensive items, drifting toward the middle'.

Since you know the standard behaviour of customers most of the time, why not instead mix up your menus completely.

The same thing happens in all kinds of dining situations. Instinctively, diners look to the middle of the menu. And if your high-contribution items are there, your profitability can get a massive boost.

Just this one minor tweak to your business, embracing Menu Engineering, can make a world of difference to your business as you pivot through a crisis. And it's far from the only thing that you can do.

**Sweetening the Deal**

Now you have learned more about what you could do with your menu. But there's another area where you can increase your bottom line – desserts.

How much do you charge for desserts right now? Is there a fixed price, or do you define it based on costs or other factors?

In the vast majority of cases, businesses do the latter. It makes sense because you'll obviously price the desserts that cost more to make higher than others.

But this is actually another common mistake that you might want to avoid. What I suggest is that you price all your desserts equally. For example, price them all at $12, $14 or $16, no matter how much they cost you.

The key here is to set the price so that it's reasonable and appealing to your customers. Some of your desserts will make you more money, while others will have a lower contribution.

But this doesn't matter as much since you are selling more now as dessert will become a reasonable add-on for many more diners, and the sale is increasing your average check. Plus, the dessert items with a higher contribution will more than make up for those that bring you less money, and you can certainly list those in the middle of the dessert menu!

This simple technique is very similar to the Moët et Chandon test. You're making money on those desserts anyway, so there is no reason to overprice them making them an unattractive offer. Remember that it's all about selling as many high-contribution items as you can. Plus, the more you sell, the less they cost you to make, as you are able to benefit from volume buying of ingredients! Now, that is Sweetening the Deal!

# *Stay on Top of Your Numbers*

There are many key reasons to understand your financials in-depth and why it is such an important pillar. First and foremost, it will give you a much higher degree of control over your business, which you will find essential in times of crisis. Your financials hide a wealth of opportunities to pivot and take your business in the direction that will ensure you survive and thrive through the challenges.

These are but a few of the improvements that you can make. The more you learn and understand, the more you'll make your hospitality business more immune to crises. That's the power of understanding how numbers affect your business.

So, if you haven't already, you'll want to make creating monthly P&L statements a habit to stay on top of your numbers. With time, this will become more natural and eventually they can be the best tools you use to better understand and manage many aspects of your business.

But how can you predict the results of those decisions before you firm them up in your plans to pivot your business? Keep reading!

CHAPTER FIVE

# *Pillar #3 – Create a Forecast to Predict the Future*

We all remember the Global Financial Crisis (GFC) that began in 2008 and lingered until as late as 2012. It was one of the worst crises in modern times, especially for hospitality businesses. Investors, business owners, and the majority of the general public took a massive financial hit. Pacific Restaurant Group Ltd (PRG Ltd) was no different.

At the time, I was serving as an Executive Director and as Financial Controller of PRG Ltd. While the GFC had less of an effect on Australia than many other countries, it impacted businesses in significant ways. There was undoubtedly much less money being spent on premium dining, according to a BIS Foodservice report. 'There is a noticeable "trade-down" effect that occurs in any economic downturn', explained Sissel Rosengren, Head of BIS Foodservice, a division of BIS Shrapnel, 'As a result, fast food chains are on the increase and are now the dominant force....'

PRG Ltd owned restaurants in locations around Australia including in Melbourne, on Flinders Lane in the CBD. The location was initially branded as Kingsleys Steak & Crabhouse but was converted to our newest brand, Chophouse, following its success in Sydney.

Partially due to the financial chaos caused by the GFC, the restaurant was sold at a substantial loss and the failure threatened our company's well-being. One of the first tools we used during this tough time was a financial forecast that would show us the right direction to move in. We needed to know exactly how much funding would be required to ensure that the PRG Ltd would not only survive but would thrive in the long run. We'd lost nearly $2 million on that restaurant so we had to bounce back as quickly as possible.

Part of my job was to create solid financial forecasts that our Board and auditors, KPMG, could rely on to formulate a plan for the future. We needed to know immediately the right mix of raising more capital and what we would generate in free cash flow from operations to ensure the company's stability.

Working with a very dedicated Board, we were able to raise money from our shareholders using that forecast and execute an operational pathway which not only allowed PRG Ltd to survive and pivot through that crisis but also thrive and go on to sign the master franchise agreement with Jamie Oliver International. Ultimately, it's what allowed PRG Ltd to eventually be sold to the Keystone Group in 2013.

Without those sound financial forecasts, we would not have been able to create a viable plan. The forecasts allowed PRG Ltd to push through one of the biggest financial crises in history and come out on top.

No matter what challenges your hospitality business is going through, a sound financial forecast is a key pillar to help you pivot through. Whether you need to raise money from investors, borrow it from a bank, or plan to trade through, you'll know how through forecasting and planning.

I'll talk about business planning in detail in the next chapter, but since forecasting is the foundation of planning, I'd like to discuss why you must get very good at it, and how to!

# *Five Reasons Why Forecasting Is Critical for Success*

Forecasting is an essential aspect of running a successful hospitality business. But it's in times of crises when you must pivot that its importance truly shines.

But why is this true? What does forecasting do that makes it so vital?

## 1. Setting the Course for the Future

You cannot create an effective business plan without forecasting. If you can't predict the outcomes of your decisions, there's no way of knowing if you're moving in the right direction. You'd be forced to guess and experiment quite a bit, which might end up costing you at a time when cash flow is tight.

Forecasting is about predicting the future using the past instead of hoping for a successful one. It allows you to test and compare multiple strategies and their outcomes. Ultimately, it enables you to define the roadmap out of a crisis.

As you go about making meaningful changes, you'll face obstacles and opportunities. If you don't have a clear budget and forecast, you can't get to where you want to be with confidence. So, before you start thinking about introducing innovative pivots to your business, a prediction is a must.

## 2. Meeting Financial Requirements

Initiating pivots may come at a cost. And more often than not, that cost has not been spent previously in your historical P&Ls. You'll have to manage your finances very wisely to ensure that you can reach your goals without overspending.

You need an accurate overview of the resources that your business needs to pivot. Be it working capital for operational cash flow or investment capital to innovate your operations, you need to know exactly how much it takes to make a change and what the most likely outcome will be.

Plus, if your pivot includes expanding or making significant capital expenditures in your business, you might need external financing including bank finance or bringing on additional investors. There's no way of knowing how much you need without a well-tested forecast. Also, investors and banks won't trust you with their money if your estimates are not sound. And normally, you won't be able to apply for bank funding without a forecast. So, to meet your financial needs to pivot through, you must put effort into accurate estimates.

## 3. Making Wise Management Decisions

Forecasts are the BEST resource to base your business decisions on. They are the fuel you need to make management-level decisions.

Why are forecasts so critical for making management decisions?

Because your decisions ultimately boil down to how well you know your business. And as I explained in the previous chapter, all the information that you need is in the numbers. Numbers don't lie.

Accurate forecasts will give you a deeper understanding of your business' health into the future. When you arrive at decisions based on hard evidence instead of gut feelings, you can push through crises much more effectively.

## 4. Controlling Your Cash Flow

You have all heard the saying 'cash is king'. When it comes to cash flow, there are two possible scenarios: Either you control it by making well-informed decisions, or it controls your business and limits your pivoting opportunities. Cash is the lifeblood of every business, and hospitality is no different. If you don't have enough cash on hand, or how much you will need to get through a crisis, going through it may be quite a financial struggle.

With accurate forecasting, you can gain full control over your cash flow and make sure that this doesn't happen. Consequently, you'll be able to manage your operations and any necessary changes much more effectively.

## 5. Make it a Team Effort

Forecasting helps everyone get on the same page when it comes to your processes and goals. As a collaborative effort, it brings together all relevant information and people. Because of this, everyone can participate in predicting the future and understanding their role in it.

There are very few things as necessary as this in a crisis – bringing all stakeholders together. If your processes get too disrupted without a forecast to guide you, your business risks facing higher future losses than the crisis itself created. And you can avoid this easily by ensuring that your operations remain as seamless as possible with a forecast in hand to navigate the pivots.

## 6. Measuring Progress

Later in the book, I'll show you how to make sure that you stay on course when you set a goal. But for now, trust me that forecasting is the basis of making this happen and is your best guide towards the desired outcome.

How so?

When you forecast, you get benchmarks against which you can measure your results. Plus, as you go about creating a detailed plan and executing it, you'll return to the forecast regularly. By doing so, you'll see how the actual results compare to the predicted ones. And if there's a gap, you'll know where to take corrective action to take and get back on track.

# *Steps to Creating a Sales Forecast*

As you can see, there are many valid reasons to get serious about forecasting, especially during a crisis. Even when you're not in a crisis, an accurate sales forecast is an invaluable part of achieving your business goals.

But what does it take to create a solid forecast? Here are the steps that you need to follow:

## 1. Gather Your Data

In the last chapter, I explained the importance of P&Ls. Now is the time to utilise that critical resource. In fact, to make the most accurate forecast, it is best to have 2-3 years of historical P&L in hand alongside your current financial information.

Without an understanding of the past and present, it will be difficult, if not impossible, to accurately predict the future, especially in a crisis. The past will reveal seasonality both in revenue and in COGS and Labour, as well as any particular month where your expenses may spike or drop. This data is KEY to ensuring that you get your forecasts right, and you can test your pivots without running into an unexpected financial roadblock.

This is why the first step to creating an accurate forecast is to have as much data and information about your business at your fingertips.

Once you've gathered everything together, it's time to break it down. By doing so, you can see where the pitfalls may occur and problems may arise.

## 2. Keep it Simple

Based on your historical data, making future projections for corresponding periods might seem daunting. Let's keep it simple and start with projecting sales for every month one year ahead. For example, you'll use the changes between July 2018 and July 2019 data as a base to project July 2020 revenue. During and just after a crisis, the most important periods are the next 3, 6, 9 and 12 months. Don't worry about projecting multiple years into the future.

Also, you might want to include quarterly projections. Doing so will help you account for seasonality. Once you have your P&Ls and present data ready, it's time to calculate the year-over-year (YoY) change to inform your future goals instead of just pulling goals out of thin air.

Let's assume you have two years of revenue data from your P&Ls. In August 2018 (Year 1) you made $100,000, while in August 2019 (Year 2), revenue was $120,000. Here's how to find the YoY percentage change:

$$YoY\ Percentage\ Change = [(Year\ 2 - Year\ 1) \div Year\ 1] \times 100$$

$$YoY\ Percentage\ Change = [(\$120,000 - \$100,000) \div \$100,000] \times 100$$

$$YoY\ Percentage\ Change = 20\%$$

Repeat the process to find YoY change for revenue for each month. Note that a positive result indicates an increase, while a negative number indicates a decrease.

Once you've done the math, consider the results: Are the past few months significantly down or up in revenue from the previous year due to factors related to the crisis, or are there other reasons including seasonality? Understanding the why behind the numbers is just as important as the data itself.

Now, you can project your revenue into Year 3, which is the future period, knowing what occurred in the last two years as a base. Regardless of whether you're projecting for a percentage drop in sales due to the crisis, a modest year-over-year (YoY) increase, or you've got more aggressive targets in mind, the key is to remain realistic as situations are less predictable during a crisis.

### 3. Projecting the Immediate Future

As your business operates through a crisis, and you are coming up with ideas on how to pivot your business, you need to be considering any new lines of revenue, and if any historical revenue streams will be discontinued. I will cover making a plan in the next chapter, but in creating a forecast, you may need to include new revenue streams that are not in historical P&Ls.

You may also need to adjust your prices up or down depending on the demand. In some cases, you may have pent-up demand after a crisis but limited capacity. In that case, some fixed-priced pivots may increase your menu prices. If you have plenty of capacity but fewer diners or customers, you may need to adjust your prices down to meet the lower demand.

Either way, there's a high chance that you'll make some price adjustments to menu items and you will need to account for that in the percent growth or shrink you expect in your business during crisis recovery.

Following the same pattern as the previous section, multiply your Year 2 revenue by what % you believe your business will grow or shrink, factoring in increases or decreases to your prices.

Let's assume you believe your business will shrink by a net 10% in Year 3. Recall in August 2019 (Year 2), revenue was $120,000. Here's how to calculate your projected revenue:

> *August 2020 (Year 3) revenue projection = [(Year 2 \*(1+% growth or shrink expected)]*
>
> *August 2020 (Year 3) revenue projection= [($120,000 \*(1-10%)]*
>
> *August 2020 (Year 3) revenue projection= $108,000*

Project each month one year forward to get Year 3 revenue projections. You may decide to vary your growth or shrink %s in future months as you pivot and add innovative new revenue streams beyond the immediate future.

Now let's focus on forecasting your COGS, Labour and Operating Expenses.

### 4. Forecasting your COGS, Labour and Operating Expenses

After you've projected your revenue, it's time to factor in your COGS, Labour and Operating Expenses. And based on the historical P&L data, you can project them in the same way you projected the revenue above.

Keep in mind that some of your costs are variable based on increased or decreased sales, but many, like insurance and possibly rent, are fixed. This is where the lessons about break-even will come in handy! If you discover that your forecasts are less than break-even, you may need to seek funding from the government in the form of grants, from investors or bank financing to make it through the crisis recovery. And it's always better to know that early on so you can incorporate it into your plan!

### 5. Testing & Updating the Forecast

When you have completed the above steps to get your forecasts done, the final step is one of the most important. You need to test a range of increases and decreases in revenue percentages. As you continue reading and begin to develop your pivots to survive and thrive through the crisis, you may want to revisit your growth or shrink percentage, and possibly even create a few scenarios based on those pivot ideas.

A well-thought-out forecast is the best starting point to give you an idea of what the future holds for your business. When you have this data, you can use it to make the decisions that will keep you moving forward.

Bear in mind though, that virtually, no forecast will be 100% accurate. This is why you will likely update your projections regularly and make the necessary adjustments as your circumstance changes. And don't worry if you are having any trouble creating forecasts, your bookkeeper or accountant can be a great resource!

# *10 Tips for Creating Accurate Forecasts*

Forecasting is no easy feat and may take a few attempts to master. There are many factors that you need to take into account if you want to do it correctly.

If you haven't done much forecasting, you might find it a bit daunting especially if the steps above have you feeling challenged. So, let me give you some inside tips that will make it run smoother and ensure higher accuracy.

## 1. Focus on Collaboration

A comprehensive business forecast will address all areas of your business. And on your own, you might not be able to have all the relevant data. This is especially true as your business grows. The more you evolve, the more moving parts you'll have to handle. And you should never try to do it alone.

Rather, you should ensure collaboration between the key people for each important function, even if you are a small operation with just a few key people. They'll have a deeper understanding of their own laneways, so they can give you the numbers and insights that you need.

So, engage all relevant people in forecasting. Not only will teamwork make it much easier, but you'll also ensure that you don't miss any important data or ideas!

## 2. Have Regular Forecasting Sessions

As I mentioned, forecasting isn't something that you set and forget. Instead, it's an evolving practice that you should review regularly in your business. This lets you adapt your forecast to the changes that occur as you pivot and stay on top of them.

Still, it doesn't mean that you need to obsess over forecasting and have this constant need to analyse every number. This might consume you and burn you out. As a result, you might not be able to see everything as clearly as you should.

It's best to have forecasting sessions on a predetermined schedule. At the absolute least, you should do it once every quarter. But you'll get much better at predicting your business' future if you do it more regularly. This is why the general rule of thumb is to do it once a month. So, meet your team, business partners or bookkeeper/accountant, discuss the forecast, and don't obsess about it too much until the next session.

## 3. Don't Confuse Speculation for Opportunity

As you go about reaching the forecasted future, a lot of things will change, especially during a crisis and crisis recovery. While you'll likely face some challenges, you'll also encounter many opportunities. But this doesn't mean that you should chase every one of them.

In fact, many things that seem like an opportunity won't have solid ground. If you can't back an opportunity up with concrete evidence, it may be nothing but a wish or speculation.

So, whenever you notice an opportunity, ask yourself one thing:

*'Are there logical steps that I can take and that would make the opportunity feasible?'*

You shouldn't disrupt your plans or processes just because you've noticed something new. This is the famous 'shiny object syndrome' and it will steer you away from the correct path. If you're to make modifications to your forecast, it should be for a solid reason, for well thought-out pivots.

## 4. Beware of Any Bias

I explained that you should endeavour to work with your team, business partner(s) or bookkeeper/accountant on creating and updating your hospitality business forecast. While this brings many benefits, it also comes with certain risks. Each of those stakeholders may have different ideas and goals, and in some cases, those goals might be conflicting. As such, the data points that you use to create a forecast might not represent the whole picture.

This is why you should rely on multiple data points when forecasting. If you do, you can minimise the chance of any bias distorting the picture.

Of course, as a business leader, you should always look in the mirror first and ensure that you're not biased. You must know the difference between what you want and what's good for your hospitality business. We can all be stubborn at times, and it is important to be open to new ideas and trust the process. And this is another reason why cold data matters. Numbers don't lie, nor can they have any biases. Because of this, make any future projection based on hard evidence and multiple data points.

## 5. Focus on Customer Behaviour

You have the freedom to make any kind of projection that you want. You can make the forecast show whatever you want to see. But the numbers will only be on the mark if diners and customers continue to patronize your hospitality business. And because of this, focusing on them is vital to making sure that your forecast is accurate.

Remember the Moët & Chandon test and menu engineering that I talked about? They all came from a careful analysis of customer behaviour. This is what allowed me to make counterintuitive moves like selling Moët & Chandon at a value-for-money price and boost my sales and contribution margin. Knowing how customers behave led me to the conclusion that high-contribution items should be in the middle of the menu.

This kind of analysis is vital in forecasting. You need to predict your customers' needs and wants and test what will make them buy more and push your revenue up. You need to test what pivots they prefer, and which ones don't work. If you disconnect from your customers and their behaviour, surviving and thriving through a crisis will be very hard.

Plus, knowing your customers helps many other aspects of your hospitality business. You can define customer personas, which is critical to effective marketing. With this in mind, it's easy to see why focusing on customers makes a world of difference to forecasting and your business as a whole.

## 6. Hope for the Best, but Prepare for the Worst

A forecast is so much more than a piece of paper that paints a picture of the future. It helps you see what it is that you can expect if you try different pivots. And there isn't always a straight line between your actions and an outcome during challenging times. Rather, it's more of a range of potential scenarios that you might face.

Because of this, your forecast should include the worst- and best-case scenarios. You need to know what will happen in case things go awry and see the best outcome that you can hope for.

In the short term, always focus on what your historical P&L data show you about the recent past and present. But in the long-term, leave some room to account for the different scenarios that you might encounter in uncertain times. If you prepare for the worst, you can push through crises much more effortlessly.

## 7. Leverage Modern Technologies

Later in the book, I will talk about specific pivots. But is your business up-to-date with the tech trends in hospitality? Do you rely on your POS, other software or app to make important decisions?

If not, now's the perfect time to consider it. Long gone are the days when an Excel spreadsheet was enough to provide you with all you need to forecast accurately. Today, hospitality tech providers have developed much more sophisticated platforms and methods. If you don't leverage them, you risk falling behind competitors that do.

If you're not sure where to start, starting with cloud-based systems could be a good idea as a beginning point. If you're still not using them, you'll want to get on board as quickly as possible. They can streamline forecasting and leave much less room for error.

Also, a good forecasting platform gives you the much-needed flexibility to make all relevant adjustments in due time. It will make you more agile, which is necessary in times of crisis.

## 8. Don't Forget the Details

When it comes to forecasting, every piece of data matters and could be relevant. So, take care to avoid ignoring or overlooking small items because they seem insignificant. You should leave no stone unturned and account for everything.

Why?

Because it's those small things that can make a big difference over time. Small, added costs can chip away at your profits and make you lose a lot in the long run as you pivot. When it comes to forecasting, the devil truly is in the details.

So, don't let the big challenges or opportunities overshadow those details. Examine every item in your business, and make sure to factor it in.

## 9. Don't Be Too Rigid

As you saw in the previous section, reviewing historical P&L and present data is vital to accurate forecasts. But you'll also want to be careful about how you use that data. You shouldn't stick to it blindly and without leaving any room for flexibility.

The hospitality landscape changes rapidly. And all those crises that we've seen only speed up the process. While your historical P&L and present data are a good foundation for future decisions, you shouldn't get stuck in them.

Instead, you need to keep an open mind and address all the changes that can influence your future. The competitive market might demand that you adapt on short notice, and you don't want to wait too long.

## 10. Have Your Forecast Assessed

If you have created your forecast in-house, great work; while it may be accurate, in some cases it won't be fully complete. You might think that you've included everything in your predictions only to realise that you've missed something down the line.

For this reason, you should always have someone impartial and objective to assess your forecast. Having a fresh pair of eyes take a look at it can be highly valuable. You might get some insight that you didn't have while you were forecasting. As a result, you can make all the necessary changes quickly.

This is especially important in the beginning if you don't have a lot of experience with forecasting. And it's another situation where having a mentor can be critical to success. So, don't do it all on your own but rather have someone more experienced to help you out.

## *Prepare for the Future*

I hope that you now understand the vital importance of forecasting. As you can see, it's among the essential activities that can get you through a crisis. When tough times hit, everything might seem hectic. You might feel like you're losing your direction, and that there's no time to make any meaningful changes.

Forecasting can give you peace of mind, as you'll have an idea what to expect from the future. It will also make you understand your business on a deeper level, which is crucial to getting out of a crisis.

Forecasting isn't always easy. But it's something that you'll get much better at with time. If you do it regularly (as you should), it will become like second nature.

In time, you will understand the intertwined relationship between forecasting and your strategies. There's no doubt that the two are inseparable. A good forecast lets you develop an effective strategy for achieving your goals. And as you go about executing the strategy, you'll tweak and adapt your forecast to the results.

However, an accurate forecast doesn't guarantee a sound strategy.

This is why forecasting is a part of one of the most important pillars in any business – planning. It's what lets you leverage the forecast to create a strategy in alignment with your goals. The next chapter will explore the importance of proper planning and what it takes to do it right.

# CHAPTER SIX

# *Pillar #4 – Make a Plan (and Measure Against It)*

Crises can come on quickly and be very uncertain times for any hospitality business. But they're rarely the end of the world for you, no matter how much they feel like they might be. The crisis is out of your control, but *you* get to choose how you're going to react to it.

That brings me to what I have mentioned in previous chapters – Making a Plan. A good plan breathes certainty into your situation and shows you that it does not have to be the end of the world and that there's still a lot that you can do to survive and thrive. Your plan is your blueprint for how you're going to push through major issues and come out stronger on the other end of the crisis.

It's the plan that helped Simon Gloftis do some pretty amazing things with his businesses. He's the owner of Hellenika at The Calile and SK Steak and Oyster. And like many of you, Gloftis was forced to close both of his businesses temporarily due to the pandemic.

That's not ideal for any business owner to go through, and Simon could have allowed fear to overtake him at that moment. He'd certainly have had the same worries as you may have about whether his business could survive, and those worries could have paralysed him.

But he didn't let that happen. Simon made a plan, which he explains in his own words:

*'I want to just clear the decks, close the doors, and when we reopen, we reopen powerful, fresh and clean and welcome people with open arms and bring back the smiles.'*

He added that closing was a decision that would allow him to come back even stronger. He wanted to take some time to adapt and pivot to all the changes and weather the storm successfully.

Some other business owners took a different, but equal approach. Instead of closing, they chose to adapt and pivot to the new condition straight away.

For instance, Gambaro Seafood Restaurant diversified with Gambaro 2 Go, a takeaway service. Co-owner John Gambaro decided to add a wide variety of dishes to his click-and-collect service and, of course, he complied with all relevant regulations!

*'All our staff will be temperature-checked, regularly (and) if you want to come in and pick up, we'll practise social distancing,'* he said.

From family meals to diet-specific foods, Gambaro brought all of the restaurant's most popular dishes to customers. Gambaro had a plan for his restaurant that meant it could keep serving customers even during a crisis.

Angelica Jolly, co-owner of Alchemy, is another hospitality hero who decided to do the same. She launched Alchemy To You, an innovative gourmet grocery service.

Jolly said that she couldn't believe it when she saw a massive lack of produce in stores. She told her husband that they should start providing groceries for people who wanted to keep eating healthy.

Alchemy To You began offering fruits, vegetables, dry goods, and protein foods from local suppliers. She chose the suppliers that usually serve high-end restaurants and whose trade had also slowed down, which means she's creating a positive change for everyone involved, from the supplier to the consumer.

*'If this can help the suppliers, and I can bring on staff to pack, then the customer wins, suppliers win and so will our staff,'* she said.

If you need more examples of successful pivots, look no further than City Winery and BrewDog.

Both businesses leveraged their retail license to start selling in stores and create another stream of income.

Plus, BrewDog began offering delivery through Deliveroo and UberEats. City Winery did a similar thing, with excellent results.

The owner, Adam Penberthy, reported that they'd receive an online order every half an hour on average.

All of the above are great examples of business owners with the right mindset. None of them let the pandemic bring them down or threaten their success.

They realised that it was only another change that required adapting to.

Of course, all these businesses took a hit. But they bounced back rapidly, thanks to proper planning.

My point is this…

Your hospitality business has many options. There's always a way forward – you just need to choose a direction to pivot and create a plan.

# Creating Your Plan – The Key Steps

In the time of crisis, or any change for that matter, your comfort zone is the most dangerous place to get stuck in. If you stick to the old ways of doing business, you'll get left behind. There's a high chance that you won't make it and your business will fall by the wayside while those who adapted, innovated and pivoted overtake you.

Because of this, thinking outside the box is critical to coming out on top. Every business that survives a crisis and thrives afterwards does so because of innovative thinking.

This makes a lot of sense. The thinking, the process, the operations that worked in the past do not always get results in times of crisis. Whenever the landscape shifts, you must take charge and adapt to what the market demands, whether that's reduced capacity or reduced demand.

This does not necessarily mean that you must reinvent the wheel or introduce any groundbreaking innovation to make this happen. I've seen restaurant owners make just the slightest of changes to their processes and succeed. But most have used some form of innovative technology or process change in their success.

So how do you initiate those changes? Here are some of the main steps that you need to take:

## 1. Know What Your Customers Want

Amid the coronavirus pandemic, many businesses had no idea what to do. And the main reason for this was that they didn't understand how their customers' needs and wants changed because of the new circumstances surrounding them. When all the pandemic social distancing and lockdown restrictions got enforced, the only thing that some business owners could think to do was close their doors, without a plan, and hope for the crisis to blow over quickly.

That's not the approach to take, as I showed you right at the beginning of this chapter. The business owners I mentioned knew that the pandemic wasn't going to stop them from providing services to their customers. They knew that customers still wanted what they had to offer, their brand, their service, and their wonderful food and beverage. So, it was only a matter of finding new ways to provide it.

Takeaways, self-delivery and app deliveries were an obvious choice. Even when people could eat out, they were afraid to. But they still wanted to enjoy their favourite meals and drinks. Add the fact that the majority of people worked from home, and you can see why takeaways, self-delivery and app deliveries got massively popular.

I recommended to any restaurateur who called for my advice that they adjust their operations to takeaways, self-delivery and app deliveries, grocery and bespoke cooking experiences for diners. And many of those who did achieve great results. They quickly understood the customers' needs and figured out an innovative way to meet them.

One great example was Stephen Mercer, of Mercer's Restaurant in Eltham, Victoria. Stephen and his wife Ute created a fine dining takeaway experience where diners were invited to watch Stephen via social media for lessons on home preparation to make sure dinner was served at a restaurant standard.

*'We thought this was a little bit different, a bit unique. A night out at home,'* Mercer said.

*'We're filling that niche - anniversaries, birthdays that would have been in the restaurant - they're so excited that they've got an option to celebrate somewhere.'*

These are just a few examples of what you could do when things change out of your control. A crisis doesn't mean that your customers don't need you or that they don't want your offer anymore. It just means that something in your relationship with them is changing, that their purchasing behaviour is changing. When you figure out what your customers want, the path through a crisis will become clearer.

## 2. Embrace Technology

Are you active on social media? Do you use it for selling? Do you utilise self-delivery apps like Bopple and Mr Yum or the larger delivery apps: Menulog, Deliveroo or UberEats? Have you ever used Zoom, Instagram, TikTok, SnapChat or Facebook videos to connect with diners and customers? If not, you're potentially missing out on a massive opportunity to connect with them.

Many business owners feel like their main job is to draw customers towards them, strictly for dine-in. But this isn't the whole truth. What you may want to be thinking about, as customer behaviour changes in a crisis, is where your customers are going. You must position yourself in front of them if you want to remain relevant during and after a crisis. A recent study published in the British Journal of General Practice concluded: it takes an average of just 66 days for a new customer behaviour to become automatic.

So, many restaurateurs don't even think about embracing new sales or marketing channels. Or worse, they think that it's a waste of time and energy or too much of a change to the dining experience. They don't realise just how big of a mistake this is. Customer habits have changed and will continue to change, especially through a crisis. By not meeting your customers where they are, you risk losing them to the competition that will.

Progressive businesses make an effort to learn where their target audience spends their time. And they use this knowledge to put themselves in front of the customers' minds and stay there. If you want to survive and thrive in the long run, you need to do the same.

Technology can also help you in your business to streamline your operations.

Take onboarding, rostering and time & attendance software like Deputy or foundU as examples. Hospitality business owners know very well how tedious rostering and time & attendance can be or how complex payroll regulations can be. So, why not let a program take care of it for you and save you a lot of headache?

A capable rostering and time & attendance platform can optimise shift times, handle swaps and time-off requests, manage your legal award and payroll requirements and allow you to focus on managing your business and selling.

Similarly, digital inventory tracking, like options from Xero, is quickly becoming a new norm. It allows you to have an accurate overview of your inventory and maximise your efficiency. You can reduce waste, manage your inventory better, and save quite some money in the long run.

Many hospitality businesses have been using reservation management software like The Fork and OpenTable for years. And many of those software providers have continued to innovate to provide POS integration, waitlist management and greater restaurant visibility.

Of course, these are only a few examples of the many technologies that could prove invaluable especially during crises and as you future-proof your business. So, if you haven't already, you'll want to think about adopting them sooner rather than later, as your customers look to their smartphones for your business.

## 3. Focus on Convenience

Today, diners and customers have more options than ever before. Even though markets tend to consolidate through and after a crisis, in hospitality, the competition is fierce so you need to do everything in your power to set yourself apart.

Of course, you'll do that with your unique dining experience, excellent service and food & beverage quality. But in many cases, you'll have to take it a step further. Instead of the unique products and services that you provide, you'll need to focus on *how* you do it. More specifically, you need to provide your customers with convenience.

Out of all the types of businesses in hospitality, I want to single out restaurants and cafes for doing a fantastic job when it comes to this. During the pandemic, and thanks to timely lobbying, they were among the quickest to adapt and start offering deliveries of alcohol.

Even outside of a crisis, I often order wines and alcohol online. As a busy professional I rarely go to the shops, as I find them to be less convenient, but also with social distancing and long lines, it has become even harder. Many of your customers may think and behave the same. When I'm planning a dinner party at home or after a long day, why take the time to go out and buy a bottle or case of wine or pre-mixed cocktails when I can have them delivered while supporting my local restaurants and cafes at the same time?

This ties back to the importance of keeping up with new technologies. Your customers certainly know that smartphones are the norm and they want those new solutions to make their lives easier. By leveraging modern technology, you can make this happen for them. And trust me – they'll be willing to pay for this.

So how convenient would you say your services are? Have you embraced any or all of the technologies mentioned above or others to make your customers' experience with you smoother and convenient? If not, this is definitely something that you should focus on in the future as you pivot through a crisis.

## 4. Work Out How to Target Customers

Where do your customers come from and who is your customer? How do you encourage them to keep visiting? Do you know the ideal customer demographic to invite to your hospitality business in the first place?

Targeting is critical to the success of any business and is even more critical as you pivot through a crisis. And in an industry as competitive as hospitality, you really need to get good at it. You want to form a base of loyal customers that will love your business and keep coming back.

But, how?

The first thing that you need to do is figure out your brand, your offering and your service area. This will tell you what kind of customers you should target.

For example, if you're a suburban coffee shop, there's no reason to target customers who live further than 4km or so away. It's highly unlikely that people will travel longer than this to visit you unless your service offering and brand are phenomenal and unique. For that reason, you should focus on local customers and build a strong relationship with them while you market your unique brand and service offering to garner customers from a bit farther away.

On the other hand, if you're an iconic restaurant on the waterfront or CBD area, you may want to broaden your reach much further to draw in domestic visitors from your state and beyond, as well as international tourists. Your targeting mechanisms will be slightly different than suburban locations.

Once you determine which broad category you fall into, it will be clearer what kind of customers you should target.

Knowing your target demographic will then help shape your decision on how much you're willing to spend to acquire each customer in that demographic. Marketing can be quite costly, so you need to crunch the numbers and maximise every dollar that you invest in it. I'll touch on this a bit more later in the chapter.

## 5. Understand Your Own Brand

There are countless tips on how to pivot your business through a crisis. And while many of them are universally applicable, it doesn't mean that every hospitality business will benefit from them equally.

As I explained, there's no one perfect way to run a successful hospitality business. You need to know how to choose the things that will work for you specifically. And for that to happen, you must understand your own brand.

First, you need to look at your numbers and get a deep understanding of them. Your financials tell an accurate and objective picture of your business' health. And when you understand them, those numbers can show you opportunities to pivot.

Next, you must know your brand and how the audience perceives it, and how they will continue to perceive it as you branch out and pivot to new revenue channels. While you position yourself uniquely in front of your customers to stand out from the crowd, it will be critical to maintain your brand identity that you have become so famous for.

And finally, you need to know your processes to identify the main areas of improvement. Maybe you already use some modern technologies but lack other solutions that can make you more efficient. Maybe you've already started offering takeaway, self-deliveries, or large app deliveries and you need to tighten up the process.

Before you can make a meaningful change, you must know your business down to the finest details. And then, see the direction in which you could move to evolve and succeed even further.

# Developing a Marketing Plan

Marketing is vital to business success. And yet, it's one of the first things that many hospitality businesses cut back on when they face a crisis. With so many challenges to work through, you might think that you don't have enough time or money to focus on marketing.

But thinking like this could be a costly mistake. As outlined previously, your customers don't disappear when you face a challenge. They're still there, and they expect you to have a plan to nurture your relationship with them. To assure them that you are still there and working through the problems. Otherwise, you risk losing them for good.

Most hospitality businesses engage in at least a few forms of marketing, usually social media and possibly EDMs. But do you have an actual marketing plan? Or do you randomly promote yourself on social media and only advertise in-house?

Unfortunately, many business owners do the latter. Most hospitality business owners now realise they need at least a Facebook and Instagram page. And they may even realise the need to promote on Google with their business listing. As a result, many business owners do all the basic things without actually scratching the surface.

But if you want to push through crises effectively and build strong relationships with your customers, you'll have to go beyond this. You need a clear and detailed marketing plan. So, here's how to create one:

**1. Set an Objective**

Marketing is much less effective if you are not sure why you're doing it in the first place. Without objectives, it's nearly impossible to gauge if your marketing is working.

While you may notice some general improvements in your business, the results may be too vague or too untraceable to know if you're marketing your hospitality business the right way.

Because of this, the first step towards creating a marketing plan is to set an overarching objective, while keeping it simple.

Generally speaking, an objective can be one of the three main things:

- Attracting new customers
- Increasing the average spend of customers
- Encouraging repeated visits/orders

Obviously, you want to achieve all of the outcomes listed above. But right now, what's the priority for your business type? If you're a new business that has just opened before, or even during, a crisis, you might need to spread the word and attract new people quickly to survive. And if you're an established business, all three objectives might be required as you navigate the crisis with some experience under your belt, but the last two are the most critical.

You know your business better than anyone, so you know what your business priority is. Each objective will require a specific marketing strategy, so use it to set the course for your future marketing efforts.

## 2. Define Specific Goals

When you have an objective, you need to pin it down by turning it into specific goals. This allows you to set the right metrics to track to ensure you stay on the right path. Plus, it gives you the clarity that you need to execute an effective strategy.

For example, if your objective is to bring in new customers, knowing exactly how many you need is essential. Your goal might be 300 new customers in the next three months. Or you might want to increase your customers' average spend from $40 to $48.

Whatever your goal is, make sure that it's specific and that it has a defined timeframe. Also, while you should always be ambitious, you should also be realistic. If your average spend is $20, you can't expect this number to go to $50 all of a sudden.

So, have clear, measurable, and realistic goals before you start marketing. This way, you'll know if your strategy is working. And if not, you'll know what corrective measure you need to take.

## 3. Define Your Target Audience

At first glance, defining a target audience for a hospitality business might seem a bit limiting. After all, ideally, you should have as many people coming in as possible and it may sound counterintuitive to focus on one specific group of people.

But from a marketing perspective, this is exactly what you should do. And while your hospitality business might have all demographics of diners coming in, there has to be a defined customer persona. This is critical for any brand, no matter the industry. And your hospitality business must absolutely have a clear brand that will set it apart from the crowd.

Without a customer persona, you'll market to everyone. As a result, you won't connect to anyone – not on a deeper level, at least. Instead, you might have many surface-level relationships. And in the long run, this will harm your business.

This is especially true in times of crisis, and its aftermath, during recovery. Your objective is to build a loyal customer base that will keep patronizing your business despite natural disasters, pandemics or other crises. This is exactly what targeting does. It allows you to form stronger relationships with customers who'll stay with you even in tough times. Customers who believe in your brand.

This behaviour was and remains especially true during crises like the pandemic. With the level of uncertainty, many customers have been reluctant to experiment and explore in new communities. Rather, they tended to stick to the places and brands that they trust and love visiting.

To target and acquire customers like that for your business, you must understand your business and brand. By doing so, you can define the voice that will resonate with your ideal customers. When defining your target audience, you must attempt to predict what they want from your hospitality business, going well beyond traditional demographics such as their gender or age.

You may want to consider their hobbies and interests as it relates to your business. What food and wine-related activities do they do in their free time? What food blogs do they read and what social media accounts do they use? How much do they earn and how do they spend their disposable income?

When you answer all the relevant questions, create the customer food & wine persona. While you can have multiple personas, they should share similar traits. You need to have a specific food & beverage persona that you'll focus your marketing efforts on. This way, your target audience can relate to your brand and connect to it more deeply.

## 4. Identify Your Customers' Needs

Once you have decided your target customer and their specific food & wine persona, it's time to align the marketing of your brand offering to their needs and wants. You'll use this knowledge as a central part of your marketing efforts. After all, hospitality businesses exist to meet their customers' food & beverage needs.

For this reason, 'why' is the key question of marketing. Why would someone want to enjoy your food and beverage, and how can you convey to them why they should?

For example, let's say that you're a private event catering business. Your target audience is mid-life professionals who live busy lives and don't have much free time to handle catering on their own. They enjoy hosting frequent social gatherings, and they're ready to pay for someone to handle the catering.

So why would they pick your event catering business?

In this situation, you will need to market the 'why'. Stand out from your competition on the channels you use for marketing showing relevant media, verbiage and images to target that demographic that is less concerned about their spend; examples of how you can take the work off their plate and give them peace of mind, making sure that the last thing that they have to worry about is catering. Wording about food & beverage quality and bespoke service levels will show you'll deliver exactly what they expect, and that they won't have to struggle on their own.

Doesn't this sound much better than 'We provide catering.'?

Rarely do customers just buy products or services without a purpose – customers usually buy solutions. When a diner sits down for a meal, coffee, a wine or a beer with a mate, they want some time to unwind, socialise, or create meaningful memories. You must play to these, be aware of these psychological needs when marketing. It's how you show people the true value of your offer beyond the product or service.

So, once you know your customer's food & beverage persona(s) you can move on to the next step, where you'll fulfil that need.

## 5. Define Your USP

What sets your brand apart from the crowd? What is unique about your business that ensures it's not just another food and beverage operation?

If you can't answer this clearly or quickly, it means that you haven't quite found your unique selling proposition (USP). Every business has one, so it's just a matter of identifying yours or being able to articulate it more clearly.

For some businesses, it may be an exclusive menu or wine list. You might source your produce from places or supply chains that your competitors don't have access to. Or you might focus on the atmosphere of your restaurant and have some unique elements. You may have a special style of service that is unique to only your business. A USP can be any of these or could even be something as simple as a specially designed space that your target audience will love.

Your business has something original or many special touches that are unique to your vision, and you must play to those strengths if you want to rise above the crowd and build a base of loyal customers.

So, take a close look at your business and find your USP, or take time to define it more clearly to your target customers. And then, pair it with what I've noted above so you are ready to take the final step.

## 6. Create Your Campaign

You have identified your objective and goals. You know better who your audience is, what they need and want, and how you can provide it in a unique way. Now it's time to sum all that information up and turn it into a campaign.

The first thing that you'll have to consider is the platform that you'll use. Will you use a targeted EDM, go on social media, pay for Google ads, or use more traditional media like print, radio or television?

Of course, none of these is mutually exclusive. You can, and should, use multiple mediums to reach your customers. Remember that it all boils down to knowing where they are and meeting them there. Meeting your customers where they are is one of the most important lessons to learn in the hospitality business. Each location will be unique in the medium customers use, from more modern in CBD's to more traditional in regional areas. Do what works best for your area.

Next, you'll need to figure out your marketing budget. This is yet another reason why you should know your numbers. You can see how much free cash flow you have, and how much you can allocate to marketing. In a time of crisis, when cash flow is short and the situation is uncertain, cutting marketing could mean cutting your business off from customers' minds. Out of sight, out of mind, they say, so be very mindful when making a forecast that you retain some level of marketing to push through.

To ensure that you don't overspend, you'll have to define the metrics that you'll measure your results against. You'll do this based on the goals that you've set and the type of campaign that you go with. Figure out your key success indicators and measure your progress all throughout the campaign.

Now, bear in mind that marketing isn't static or set in stone. Much like every aspect of your business, it will evolve. As you execute your strategy, you'll gain many insights that you'll want to use to tweak the campaign.

No plan is perfect, so always leave some room for flexibility. Stay on the lookout for new opportunities while staying focused on your goals. With time, your strategies will become more effective, and they'll get you to where you want to be.

# *Be the Jet Engine (Not the Propeller)*

I have told this story many times through the years, but with the perfect storm of drought, fires, floods and pandemic that Australia experienced in 2020, it holds even more truth as we accelerate change.

At the beginning of WWII, all planes had propellers. But by the end of the war, jet engines became the new norm. The entire aviation industry had to pivot due to a crisis that called for innovative solutions. It was not easy, and I'm sure that it was a shock to the traditional propeller industry, but the rapid change led to the vast network of travel and transport we have today. No one could imagine a world functioning as it does without jets today.

This is a perfect analogy of how the business world works. When faced with major crises and challenges, your focus should be finding solutions that meet the new circumstances. In other words, you need to be the jet engine instead of a propeller that quickly became a thing of the past, and secondary to jets.

Proper planning helps you pivot the right way and stay on top of change. Instead of being ruled by the crisis, you take the wheel and start adapting. If you are open-minded, agile and flexible, your business will be more stable as the crisis passes.

Many businesses have pivoted successfully during the COVID-19 pandemic. Take Fix Wine Bar + Restaurant in Sydney as an example. When the coronavirus started spreading in Australia, they took a hit like most hospitality businesses. In the words of Stuart Knox, the bar's operator:

*'Business has been steady throughout the last few weeks, but on Monday we had all our bookings cancel through March. I've been in the industry long enough to comfortably say business will go downhill very quickly from here.'*

Knowing that things were about to change, Knox decided to make some changes as well. He designed a takeaway menu for office workers who couldn't visit anymore. He also brought the price of the dining voucher down from $200 to $150 for $200 worth of value. They also listed on the self-delivery app, Bopple, to provide another method to reach their target audience. And when bums on seats were allowed once again in Sydney at a reduced capacity, Stuart was elated.

*'We're fully booked,'* says Stuart-Knox, the wine bar turned restaurant's jovial owner. *'Ten people, every 90 minutes.'*

Fix Wine Bar + Restaurant had a very successful pivot. And this is because the team reacted quickly. They made and executed a well-thought-out plan that helped the business survive the tough times. Pair the right mindset with a good plan, and you can do the same.

## *Prepare for Changes*

A good plan is critical to success and a very important pillar to pivot your business. It helps you ensure that crises don't knock your business away from the right path. After all, there's a reason why they say that a good plan is half the job done.

When creating your plan, don't underestimate the importance of marketing. Go through all the steps that you saw here and be sure not to overlook anything. Get to know your audience on a deeper level, and then find out how you can connect with them with your USP.

And finally, whichever plan you might be executing, don't forget the importance of technology. Whether you're marketing or changing your processes, modern solutions can be your best friend.

Now, I know what you might say: *'That's nice and all, but high-end technological solutions cost a lot!'*

Well, let me help you address that problem in the next chapter.

CHAPTER SEVEN

# *Pillar #5 – Create New Streams of Revenue*

There are numerous amazing and innovative examples of hospitality businesses pivoting to adapt during the pandemic crisis. Business owners realised they could not operate 'business as usual', as doing so would threaten their survival.

Undoubtedly, the main pivot that hospitality businesses made was switching to the takeaway, self-delivery and app-based models. This made perfect sense, as it was the only way to reach people during the lockdown and it allowed the hospitality business to continue to operate even though restrictions did not allow for in-venue dining.

But it was no easy feat.

So many of the restaurants that made this pivot hadn't ever offered takeaway or delivery before. IBIS World indicated in 2019 that about 8% of Australian dining was some method of delivery, and during the peak of the crisis it approached 100% in some areas. It has returned to the 25-30% range and is expected to remain at that level into the future as diners habits have changed. Thanks to lobbying efforts, hospitality businesses were also allowed to offer takeaway and delivery alcohol.

Due primarily to the agility of the hospitality industry, around two-thirds of all hospitality businesses stayed open and continued trading during the pandemic. And many of those who had to shut down temporarily at the start of the pandemic reopened to get back on track.

The industry saw the pandemic, or any crisis for that matter, for what it really was – an opportunity for hospitality businesses to open up new streams of revenue that they've never considered before and may have even rejected previously. It was an opportunity for so many to reassess their models in an effort to survive and with an aim to thrive.

Aside from bums on seats, hospitality businesses need to be agile during and after any crisis to identify new channels to provide them with valuable sources of revenue while ensuring they continue to support their customers in the best way possible. By doing so, they can survive that crisis, keep their employees in jobs, and thrive into the future.

So, have you ever considered new revenue channels for your hospitality business, or have you started to pivot and want to know more?

I'm 100% sure that there are at least a few ways that you could pivot and create a new revenue stream for your business. Several, in fact. No matter what kind of hospitality business you operate, there are many valuable add-ons that can bring tremendous value to customers, that help keep them connected to your business and brand.

In turn, you'll get extra revenue to weather the storm and thrive beyond it. By doing so, you're not just finding a way to survive during a crisis. You're also building a stronger business that will be able to thrive when you come out on the other side.

# *Other Streams of Revenue to Consider*

When thinking about pivoting, many business owners believe that they need to make massive changes, which may leave them feeling so overwhelmed by the challenge that they don't even try to make a change.

But in reality, even the smallest pivots can make a world of difference. You can think of each small pivot as a building block. Stack them up one-by-one and you'll find that lots of small changes can lead to much bigger results.

So, let's outline some of the main pivots, both small and big, that your hospitality business could make both during and through a crisis.

## 1. Create Digital Menus

While digital menus are nothing new, they have become more prevalent during the pandemic and even encouraged by many authorities as more COVIDSafe. From a customer's perspective, digital menus can be seen as safer and more convenient, increasing their confidence.

An excellent example of a restaurant that realised this is Super Ling. It utilises HungryHungry, a popular digital menu platform. HungryHungry's founder Mike Calabro summarises the benefits perfectly:

*'Customers don't have to touch anything, and it saves the staff writing the order down and then going and putting their order into a computer. Customers ordering from their own phone also means you can track who has been in the restaurant.'*

Diners have the ability to change the language on the menu, see pictures of each menu item, order seamlessly on their own device, and even pay from the platform; all can lead to increased revenue; plus, it can improve the time on the table allowing for potentially more table turns.

Corbett and Claude is another fitting example of digital menus done right. The restaurant has QR codes on tables that customers can scan as soon as they sit down. And when they do, a digital menu pops up, allowing them to place an order.

This results in a more streamlined service that benefits both waiters and customers. It saves time and effort previously necessary to write down orders, which customers certainly appreciate. Plus, there's much less room for errors or mixed-up orders.

With all this in mind, it's easy to see why digital menus can be a fantastic pivot to your hospitality business.

## 2. Offer Self-Delivery or App-Delivery

You can certainly increase your revenue by pivoting to a delivery channel in your business. During the pandemic crisis, delivery became the largest revenue stream for many hospitality businesses. The key is determining what method of delivery is right for your business, and how frequently to utilise delivery to maximise revenue without sacrificing margin or quality.

Now, when you decide to do this, you'll face two options: You can either focus on app-based delivery through platforms like Menulog, UberEats and Deliveroo or the newest platform, Providoor, created by restaurateur Shane Delia. Or you can offer self-delivery in-house or through platforms like Bopple.

The larger app-based delivery platforms provide the benefit of convenience, national advertising, and have high customer downloads and reach. Self-delivery gives you more control over the delivery process, the customer experience and customer data. Both have pros and cons as to cost, which will depend on your specific hospitality business model, and now allow you to list any or all of your menu and set your prices on the platforms regardless of dine-in menu prices.

If you do decide on self-delivery, the logistics of it all might seem a bit daunting at first. Luckily, it shouldn't take you long to figure it out. And once you build the right framework, everything will be much more effortless.

Just ask Edouard Raymond, the co-owner of Bistro Gitan. In his words:

*'The first week we did it was chaos. But we learned from our mistakes, and this weekend we did 250 deliveries, and it worked really well.'*

The key to success with the delivery pivot is ensuring that delivery remains an incremental revenue to your core revenue channel(s) which are already getting your business over break-even. This will ensure that your margins on delivery remain high and that it is a positive cash flow pivot for your hospitality business. You also may want to utilise delivery on off-peak times, when you have fewer bums on seats, to help boost revenue outside of your normal hours or days of trade and to ensure your kitchen is not overwhelmed during your normal peak times. This will keep your service and quality at the level your customers expect.

Offering delivery through any channel can certainly incrementally increase your revenue and be a valuable pivot during and after a crisis. Once you go through a trial-and-error period, testing both types of delivery methods to see if one or both are right for your business, you can certainly see positive results.

## 3. Capitalise on Your Brand

Does your business have an online presence that you can monetise? Do you run a blog that would encourage customers to spend more time with you even when they're not visiting? If not, you're missing out on a significant opportunity with the addition of this pivot.

Food is a cultural phenomenon, especially in Australia, where dining is woven into the fabric of society. People patronize your business because they want to experience food, service and atmosphere in a way that they're unable to recreate or produce at home. They want the best teams to create dining experiences they will remember.

In other words, they are buying into your expertise, built over many years. And it's that very expertise that you can capitalise on through and after a crisis to create a new revenue stream for your business.

If you've never written articles for your website or social media, I strongly suggest that you give it a try. Start by creating a blog page where you can post exciting updates and educate your customers about your food, wine, food philosophy or history. By doing so, you'll not only teach them, but you'll also keep them more engaged. And this can pay off massively in the long run.

Little by little, you can build a loyal base of foodie fans that read your blog regularly. And there's a high chance that they'll also become your regular customers. You can use that blog to promote your new dishes, offers and many other things that will keep diners coming back.

From this perspective, your business is like any other retail business, no matter the industry. Every retail brand needs to stay connected to its customer base. In times of crisis, these are the people that keep your business afloat and ensure that you can survive and thrive post-crisis.

A perfect example was the #EatAloneTogether initiative created by Belinda Clarke, the COO of Restaurant & Catering Australia (R&CA). During the pandemic, Unilever Food Solutions (UFS) partnered with R&CA to maximise the campaign to support local restaurants on Takeaway Tuesday.

Yezdi Daruwalla, managing director of UFS, explained the objective of the campaign:

*'If we want to continue enjoying our local neighbourhood cafes and restaurants, we need to support them now so that their doors can remain open when we come out on the other side of this pandemic.'*

Thousands of people joined the initiative, helping their favourite restaurants survive the pandemic. They ordered takeout and delivery from the very places that gave them so many amazing experiences before the crisis. And as a result, those businesses created an extra stream of revenue that's proven invaluable during such trying times.

This is the power of having a loyal fan base. Diners would not have an interest in supporting their local restaurants if they weren't strongly connected to them. And it's a restaurant's brand that creates this strong connection.

To boost your brand presence and reap these benefits, you should position yourself as an expert in your market, in your area and of your food type. And blog articles are a perfect way to make it happen.

You can take it a step further and host your own podcast. Avid foodies love listening to food experts, especially if it's a specific food topic that they have an interest in. You can interview your staff and share their knowledge with your dining audience. You can also create all sorts of entertaining content that will keep your customers engaged. The key is to get started!

When it comes to capitalising on your brand, the opportunities are truly endless. So, go ahead and explore them, as doing so can do wonders for your revenue.

## 4. Become a Retailer, Wholesaler, or Even an Exporter

More and more retail stores are adding restaurants to their locations. This is especially true for those massive stores in retail precincts where shoppers want the convenience of being able to stay in-store to dine. So why not reverse this trend and add a retail component to your hospitality business?

There are all sorts of things that you can sell as a part of your retail efforts. This includes artisan tableware, merchandise, and even some special ingredients that you have. What matters is that your offer is in alignment with your brand and that your customers find it attractive.

Great examples of hospitality businesses that quickly pivoted to add a retail channel were St. Ali in Melbourne owned by Salvatore Malatesta, who opened their General Store offering 'Essential items for household, kitchen and life.', their amazing coffee line, and the St. Ali Wine Store offering 'Essential items for STAYING SANE.' And restaurateur Lino Scidone pivoted La Camera Southgate quickly adding prepared meals, Italian grocery items, and pre-mixed cocktails to help his business survive and thrive through the pandemic.

Alternatively, if you're ready to make some bigger pivots, you can become a wholesaler much like St. Ali with their coffee products. If you produce high-quality or unique products targeted to the general public, you can supply larger retailers or even other hospitality businesses. And if you want to go really big, you could even explore exporting those goods!

There is no doubt that adding retail, and possibly wholesale or export channels to your business can add much-needed revenue streams. But it can do something much more important in the long run – keep customers loyal. If customers buy your products, they're deeply interested and invested in maintaining a relationship with your business.

## 5. Focus on Bespoke Experiences

Many consumers want a fine dining experience, even when they're not able to go out. Normally fine dining is not suitable for takeaway or delivery and it's often the dine-in atmosphere which makes the entire fine dining experience whole. But some operators did not let this stop them from pivoting in the crisis!

Take Stephen Mercer as an example. He's the owner of Mercer's Restaurant in Eltham, Victoria. Pre-COVID, his restaurant was exclusively a fixed-price, dine-in, fine dining establishment. However, Stephen realised the need to pivot and provide unique bespoke experiences to those who weren't able to visit.

Because of this, he switched to a fixed-price takeout model. Elated diners would receive a takeaway box that they'd unpack and finish off with him via instructions on a Facebook video, as he also unpacked and finished off the meal from the same takeaway containers. Stephen would show clearly that takeaway fine dining could be plated and prepared much like in the restaurant and even suggested that diners light candles to help create a fine dining experience at home.

Needless to say, this kind of innovative thinking paid off not only for Mercer's Restaurant but at many establishments throughout Australia. It's a pivot that most customers would have never seen before, and many diners welcomed the opportunity to have such a unique experience when restrictions did not allow dine-in.

## 6. Offer Cooking Classes

If you already provide unique and high-quality dishes, why stop at just serving them? While this will always be at the core of your hospitality business, there's more than one way to monetise your know-how. And cooking classes can be a fantastic activity.

Just because consumers love eating out, doesn't mean that they don't want to prepare meals themselves. On the contrary, many people would love to know how to recreate some of their favourite dishes. And they are more than willing to pay a professional to teach them.

If you need an example, look no further than Maha. The restaurant offers all-inclusive cooking classes with Shane Delia, a professional chef (and also the founder of Provedoor mentioned earlier!). They host the classes in their dining room and provide value in many forms. They offer champagne and canapes on arrival, meet-and-greets, booklets, and many value-adds aside from the class.

Maha charges $250 per person for the massively popular classes, providing another revenue stream to the restaurant when it needs it the most.

Plus, with modern technology at the heart of pivoting your hospitality business, you don't even have to host these classes in your venue. You can take the classes online, which comes with a myriad of benefits.

Firstly, it's perfect for crises such as the pandemic when people can't leave their homes. Next, this can be a time when people want to pick up a new skill, which is all the more reason to offer an online class. Lastly, there's no limit to how many people can attend your class. If you promote them well, you can gain a much-needed revenue stream.

But how can you provide your customers with valuable add-ons online? You can't provide them with your service or offer meet-and-greets the same way you can in person.

There are many additional ways to fill your classes with value. These include providing the grocery items for recipes via a meal box delivered to their homes, recipe books, step-by-step recorded guides for prep, and future discounts or coupons for your venues. Not only can you give more value to your customers, but you can encourage them to visit you more once the crisis abates. So aside from this extra source of income, your dine-in may also see a future increase.

## 7. Host Special Events

When thinking about pivots for dine-in, when you may be under capacity limits or you just need new revenue streams during a crisis, it's always a good idea to mix things up a bit and bring some excitement to your hospitality business. Remember that diners aren't always just coming to your venue for food. They want to enjoy a nice experience and spend some quality time eating out.

There's a myriad of ways to leverage this and boost revenue. You could host events dedicated specifically to couples, families, or working from home business people coming together to socialise. Of course, you'll want to pay attention to your core audience here and tailor the events to them.

During the events, you should consider fixed-price menus that reduce waste and maximise contribution margin, special offers for certain times of day, have your Executive Chef greet each table personally, or add some special decorations to your space. People will have an amazing, memorable experience, which will make them loyal future customers.

You could also make certain days of the week or month dedicated to such special events. By doing so, you'd encourage customer returns and keep your new target audience more engaged. The opportunities are truly endless, so don't be afraid to let your imagination soar to host exciting events.

With special events and larger bookings, you also want to consider pre-charging for the event to protect your business. You can set a specific timeframe in which customers can cancel free of charge. And if they break this deadline, customers may have to pay a fee that you set.

In many cases, this will discourage people from cancelling altogether. But sometimes, they won't have a choice. They might be facing an emergency that prevents them from visiting. In this case, encourage them to contact you on time so that you can remove the reservation and free up the spot for new customers.

Yes, setting a cancellation fee can be a bit tricky and you might be afraid that it will put some diners off. But this is exactly where the importance of loyal customers can shine. Those who truly care about visiting your venue won't mind the fees. If you approach them from the right perspective, cancellation fees won't cause you trouble. And they can go a long way towards protecting your business during tough times and allow your special events to be a successful pivot for your business!

# *Maximise Your Revenue Potential*

How many of these pivots could you realistically implement into your business?

Each can provide the opportunity to provide a significant boost to revenue during a time of crisis. And when looking forward to the future, each of these new revenue streams can combine to create a business that no longer relies on a single service channel. Your hospitality business will be less vulnerable to external pressures and crises that may have held you back.

But if making extra money from your venue with pivots is possible, why do so many business owners struggle during and after a crisis?

It's because they work *in* their business instead of *on* it. Ultimately, creating new revenue streams requires you to take a step away from the business so that you can implement changes to how it operates. Remember that as a business owner, your job is to be a leader. You need to think strategically and create plans instead of getting too bogged down in the small everyday details. You only have so much brain power and energy, so do your best to use it wisely to drive your business forward.

Are you considering adopting any of the above changes? If not, it's time to do some thinking and find out what's best for you to conquer this critical pillar. Pair this with the planning tips outlined in the previous chapter, and you can set yourself up for the future, post-crisis.

Still, a plan is only an idea if you don't execute it. So, how do you do it right? That's what I'll show you in the next chapter.

# CHAPTER EIGHT

# *Pillar #6 – Execute the Plan*

Earlier, I discussed Pacific Restaurant Group Ltd (PRG Ltd) and the work I did with Kingsley Smith to transform the Group from a simple idea into the first full-service public restaurant group in the country. That vision began to reach its fruition in 2008, and then crisis struck.

The Global Financial Crisis (GFC) hit and it couldn't have happened at a worse time for PRG Ltd. We were in a growth phase, having just opened Chophouse and the new site in Melbourne.

So, for 2020, I feel like I'm facing a familiar territory. The numerous financial and strategic challenges we faced during the GFC culminated in the sale of the Melbourne business. Naturally, this called for a major shift and a whole new plan.

I told you earlier how forecasting helped PRG Ltd pivot. But of course, it wasn't only about forecasts and plans. Putting ideas and numbers on paper does not mean a thing if you don't execute the plan!

Working with qualified industry leaders and mentors, I helped get our business out of the biggest financial crisis of the time. We had to make some major shifts in focus and strategy, which involved a great deal of risk.

Luckily, we stuck to that solid plan, and it paid off. Following the pathway we had formulated led to PRG Ltd being in a stable financial position, and eventually to Jamie's Italian Master Franchise Agreement. We'd weathered the storm, learned a great deal about our business and felt much more confident that PRG Ltd could absorb whatever crisis might come its way.

Each business PRG Ltd owned was managed by teams of the most capable people I'd ever met, and I knew that it would keep growing and evolving into something exceptional. And it did. In 2013, the business sold to Keystone Group at an astonishing multiple compared to what we'd raised in the initial IPO.

This would never have happened without effective plan execution. The plan that we created brought all the key stakeholders on board and, with their support, we were able to introduce those major positive changes.

And this brings me to one of the major challenges that you may face when trying to create change in your business. You've got to get buy-in from the key stakeholders: investors, suppliers, landlords, the Council, and most importantly the employees who help you provide your services day in and day out. Without them, any plan that you create is doomed to failure simply because you need your team to execute alongside you.

So… how do you make that happen?

# *10 Tips for Getting Buy-In from Your Employees*

Your employees know you as well as you know yourself and how you operate. They may have become accustomed to your standards and processes, and also may have settled themselves into a comfort zone. But any crisis naturally yanks everyone, you, your business and certainly your employees, out of that zone.

The same goes for any pivot or change that you attempt to introduce into your hospitality business. Some of your employees may fear that the changes you plan to execute may negatively impact their position in the business. Others might take the news about the pivot as a sign that the business is in imminent danger and they need to get out now before it collapses around them.

For these reasons, you must go above and beyond to ensure that your team understands the pivot the right way. Without this, executing your plan might be impossible. After all, the success of your business depends on your people's willingness to work towards a better future. You can't pivot your business out of a crisis and thrive on your own.

So, how do you get everyone on board with your plan? Here are some tips you should follow:

## 1. Create a Strong Pitch

If you had to present your plan to investors, you'd make sure that it was airtight. You'd leave no room for doubt so that you get buy-in with very few questions or concerns. Well, you need to do the same thing when talking to your employees.

I already mentioned that you should involve all the key stakeholders in the planning process, of which your key management team is critical. So, before you even get to the execution stage, you'll need them to be ready to plan all the necessary changes and pivots. They'll do their best to create a plan that will let your business push through.

Plus, it will make it much easier to get other employees and stakeholders into the right mindset when it comes to the change. Your key management team will help you spread the message about the changes further and support you. As a result, it will be much easier to unite everyone under the same goals.

For all of the above to happen, you must have a powerful pitch to that key team. You need to clearly show that change is a good thing and that they should see it as an opportunity to take the business to the next level.

Within the pitch, you need to address the following:

- Why the pivot needs to happen
- The main goals of the change
- What the benefits will be

It's vital that your key management team believes in the plan and its positive outcome. If you can make this happen, you'll be unstoppable in pivoting your hospitality business.

## 2. Listen to Feedback

The last thing you want is to make your whole team feel like you're imposing or forcing any changes on them. Rather, what you should do is make sure that they feel heard and understood.

The thing is your team members might already have some ideas on the positive changes that need to happen. This is especially true if they've been working in your business for a longer time. As they got better at their job, they likely figured out what would make it better. And it's vital to listen to their suggestions.

The main benefit of this will be that everyone working in your business will feel respected and appreciated. And this is essential to getting the buy-in that you need.

But also, you might hear some excellent ideas on how to execute the plan or tweak it. Each employee in your business has their own valid perspective. Because of this, they can often provide valuable insight that you might not have.

So, let your whole team scrutinise the plan and make their suggestions. Of course, you don't have to accept all of them, but keep an open mind and let them see that you respect their opinion. This way, they'll be much more likely to work hard to make the changes happen.

## 3. Lead by Example

This is one of the most important lessons that every business owner can learn, regardless of the industry that they're in. You can't expect your employees to think, act and operate in a way that you're unwilling to. In other words, you must *show* your employees how to execute a plan rather than just *telling* them how.

For example, if you resist or fear change or innovative pivots, it's unreasonable to expect those around you to embrace them. Your team looks up to you as a leader and needs you to show them the way. You must accept this role and be a true leader instead of just a boss.

Teach and display to your employees discipline, honesty, and perseverance. Let them see that you know what you're doing, and show commitment to the business' well-being. When your team sees this, it will inspire them to get on board and work hard.

## 4. Explain the Roles that Everyone Will Play

During a crisis, you certainly don't want to create any additional confusion or chaos. Your employees will likely be stressed already, so it's best to make things as simple and straightforward as possible.

Plus, some pivots might be quite daunting. They might disrupt the status quo and the ways of operating that your employees may have gotten used to. You need to make sure that the changes don't seem too overwhelming.

To make this happen, you must define clear roles and responsibilities. Tell every team member about their contribution to the change. Explain what, when and how they need to do their bit. Answer their questions as best you can and give them the knowledge and tools that they need to fulfil their role.

If you do this, everyone will play their part in the pivot much more effortlessly. In addition, they'll feel valued and feel like they're a part of something bigger than themselves. And this is critical to the long-term success of your business.

## 5. Be Transparent at All Times

It will likely take time to introduce all the changes that you need to survive and thrive. You'll also have to wait for those changes to take effect. It's critical to keep your team up to date on everything that's going on.

This way, you can avoid any misinformation or gossip about the strategy and its outcome. The last thing you need is for your people to spread fearful news and lose their trust or hope in the plan.

Always be open and honest about how the changes and pivots are going. If you hit any obstacles along the way, let your team know about it. Show them what it takes to get back on track and how they can help. Motivate your employees and let them know that there's no reason for concern. When they see your honesty, your team will trust you and the strategy much more.

## 6. Provide Continuous Education and Training

If you expect your employees to change the way they're doing things, you must provide them with the necessary skill sets. Long-lasting change takes time and effort, and there has to be a strong foundation on which you'll build it.

Let's say that you were shifting your focus to pivot to deliveries. You won't serve the foods the same way you do when someone visits your restaurant to dine-in. You'll need to teach your team how to prepare and package foods in a way that will delight and impress customers. And this will likely take some education and training.

The same goes for any other change that you need to make. Everyone involved in it should upgrade their skills and knowledge base. And they shouldn't have to do this on their own. You need to provide your team with everything it needs to make the change happen and get your business back on track.

## 7. Let People Play to Their Strengths

As a leader, you shouldn't waste your time and energy on the things that aren't worth your effort. You need to know what you do best, focus on it, and let the right people handle everything else.

And you should have the same approach when it comes to delegating tasks to your employees. You need to understand their strengths and make sure that their contribution to the change matches these. Otherwise, you might stunt their growth and damage both their effectiveness and efficiency and they may feel less productive.

Now, this doesn't mean that you should let every person do only the things that they like. Everyone will have to stretch beyond their comfort zone. Still, you should always ensure that everyone does what they're best at. You know your employees, so you should have an idea of how each of them could contribute to the pivot. Delegate carefully, and you can maximise the speed of the change.

## 8. Celebrate Short-Term Wins

As explained, you'll likely have to wait a reasonable amount of time until all your changes take full effect. Your team will have to invest themselves into the pivots before they start noticing rewards.

If you make them wait to see the end result to feel accomplished, they might feel demotivated. For this reason, you must set milestones along the way. Track all the relevant metrics and let your employees see that they're making concrete, positive progress.

It doesn't have to be anything massive, just something to keep the morale high. Periodic quick wins can go a long way towards keeping people engaged in the change and motivating them to keep going.

In relation to this, you should also show your appreciation for the employees that generate those small wins. Reward them in some way and let them know that their work is highly valued. Doing so will push them to strive for more, and your whole business will see the positive effects of this.

## 9. Address Any Resistance

Despite your best efforts, you might notice some resistance to the changes in your business. Many of your employees were comfortable in the way that things worked. And when things changed, they might have felt fear or hesitant to get on board. And while they'll tell you that they're willing to help make the change, you might notice that they're not quite ready for it.

When this happens, you must address it directly and without any hesitation. Those who aren't willing to make a change may hold your business back unintentionally. At first, this might cause minor issues. But with time, those issues might snowball into major obstacles. And with so many outside problems that a crisis can bring, the last thing you need is internal struggles.

This is why you must reach out to the employees that don't fully commit themselves to the change. Your goal here is to identify their concerns and help them see the change as positive, and their contribution as essential. If you succeed, their renewed mindset will have a positive ripple effect on the other team members.

This way, you can rest assured that everyone will stay truly committed to the pivot.

## 10. Leave No Room for Complacency

In the previous points, the focus has been on what you should do when things get tough during the pivot. But what happens when everything's going well and you're making forward progress?

It's all too easy to get comfortable when you see that everything's going according to plan, but when the crisis continues to rage around you, if you get too comfortable, you risk losing your edge by getting complacent. And when that happens, your progress might stagnate, or you may even go backwards.

The same can happen to your employees. When they see the results and see you relaxing your focus as if the crisis is over, they might also lose focus. And this can be very dangerous. When you're facing a crisis, you can't afford to stop pivoting forward.

While you should definitely celebrate your achievements, don't let this rob you of the focus and your drive to keep going. As soon as you notice any complacency in yourself, snap out of it and keep working, and your team will take your lead. As I'll explain in the next chapter, change should be an ongoing part of your hospitality business. You must be ready to commit in the long run and keep evolving at all times.

# How to Execute Your New plan

If you use the tips outlined above, you should have no trouble getting your entire team invested in the new plan. And when that happens, it's time to start executing.

As I explained, a good plan really is half the job done. But it's still only a half! Without proper execution, you risk your plan being nothing more than a piece of paper in your drawer. To ensure that this doesn't happen, follow these tips for effective execution:

## 1. Don't Lose Sight of Your Metrics

In Chapter Six, I told you that setting the right metrics and benchmarks is vital to success. It allows you to define a clear course of action and ensure that you don't steer away from the path. Plus, it lets you see if your plan is solid and if there are any tweaks that you need to make.

With this in mind, tracking your key metrics is essential to pivoting. It's something that you should do continuously as you go about making those big pivots and changes.

Of course, you can't do it all on your own. There will likely be many numbers to track, so you'll need your capable team by your side. Since this is the team who've helped you create the plan in the first place, as they'll have a deep understanding of it. You'll also want to get your mentor on board, for the reasons that I explained back in Chapter Three. A mentor can help guide your pivot in the right direction, ensuring that you remain focused.

So, make progress-tracking a habit when making any important changes to your business. As a side benefit, you'll get motivated when you see the proof that your plan is working.

## 2. Focus on Accountability

At the end of the day, no one cares about your hospitality business more than you do. Because of this, you must hold yourself accountable for all the changes that you need to make. You need to assume full control and responsibility over the strategy and its outcome. This will motivate you to stay focused and committed to execution.

But if you're the only one accountable, you won't get very far. This is why you need to build this same kind of responsibility in your entire team. As I explained, you must lead by example. And accountability is one of the main things that your employees must see in you. Otherwise, they won't hold themselves responsible for the results.

Once you set clear roles that everyone will play, make sure that they understand their responsibilities. Empower each team member to give it their all to execute their part of the plan. Be sure to avoid a culture where employees pin the blame on one another, or keep score, especially during major crises. Let everyone know what you expect of them and ensure that they remain responsible for the outcome.

## 3. Have Regular Meetings

Effectively executing a new strategy relies heavily on good communication and alignment. Your whole team should understand the main objective and how their actions fit in. They should also be able to track their own progress, with your feedback.

To ensure alignment throughout the execution, meet up with your team regularly, through three meeting types.

First, you need to have daily huddles. These are short meetings that you'll use to see how the day-to-day activities are going. The meeting should last for no more than 15 minutes, as this is plenty of time to get the high-level updates and pass on new information.

You should also schedule weekly check-ins with key managers, where you'll examine last week's progress towards the plan. These meetings will run a bit longer and focus on strategy. Plan for up to an hour.

And finally, you need monthly meetings with your entire team. This is where you'll discuss different tactics and how they fall in line with the overall pivot strategy and hear feedback from everyone. It's also where you should discuss big-picture issues. These meetings may go a bit longer than an hour, as you let everyone have a say in the progress.

Depending on the scope and duration of the pivot, you can also have quarterly, or even annual meetings dedicated to the changes. What matters here is that you stay in touch with your team at all times. Otherwise, you might not notice some issues that could hinder your chances of pivoting successfully.

These meetings can also be an excellent way to keep your entire team motivated. Set aside some time in the monthly meetings to address incremental wins and the progress that you've made towards the entire plan. Doing so will keep everyone's spirits up and ensure that they stay driven and committed.

## 4. Address Individual Changes

While you pivot, it won't be just your business and processes that will change. Each of your team members may go through individual changes within the organization. Of course, the same goes for you. Being too obsessed over the changes happening in your business might prevent you from seeing those individual pivots. And this might threaten the sustainability of your pivot.

Because of this, you need to acknowledge the new rules that you and your team will play by. Some people will lose certain responsibilities and replace them with new roles. You must track how your employees adapt to these changes, and if they'll be ready to embrace them fully, and how you can help them embrace that change through professional development.

Plus, each person will transition at a different point in time. Not everyone embraces change the same way, so you'll have to keep an eye on each of your team members. As outlined before, you need to support them and provide the development and guidance they need to make the change as smooth as possible.

## 5. Stick to the Core Success Indicators

Change is rarely a straight line. There are many ways to reach any goal that you set. Just because you have a detailed plan does not mean that it can predict every future scenario. As you go about the execution stage, you'll face challenges and opportunities. Each of them might compel you to change the strategy and the direction that you're moving into.

There's nothing wrong with some flexibility. In fact, you'll have to leave some room for tweaking to account for the uncertainty that the future will bring. But this doesn't mean that you should let go of other aspects of your plan completely.

In other words, you must focus on your plan's core objectives and the indicators of progress. If you don't, you risk abandoning the original plan and ending up with a different outcome.

Once you set a plan and the main goals, maintain a laser-sharp focus on them. Should any opportunities arise, pin them for later if they don't fall in line with the original plan, or determine how they can be incorporated into your plan. You can't execute multiple strategies effectively at the same time. So, remain somewhat flexible, but always measure your success according to the predefined goals and metrics.

## 6. Don't Rush It

In a crisis, patience might not be your strongest suit. You might feel the need to pivot as quickly as possible to make sure that you stay on top instead of getting overwhelmed by the crisis. But patience is a virtue you must embrace as you pivot.

Now, it's obviously critical to adapt to changes as soon as you can. But this should never happen at the cost of your business' well-being. If you only focus on the speed of all the changes, you risk making mistakes.

Remember that the pivots that you're making should be sustainable in the long-term. You won't return to the old ways once the crisis is over. Instead, you'll build a foundation for a new way of running your hospitality business. And this takes time.

For this reason, arm yourself with patience and understand that major pivots are a marathon, not a sprint. Be meticulous with both your plan and its execution to ensure that everything you do will be viable long after the crisis passes. Empower your team to focus on the long run as well, and move slow and steady towards a more successful future.

## *Take Massive Action*

The planning can be an enjoyable and exciting start to the pivot.

It's your chance to brainstorm ideas and think up outside of the square ideas that you can try, to create an even more amazing hospitality business. That doesn't mean it's going to be easy, of course. You'll hit the occasional brick wall when you're planning, with roadblocks along the way, just like you would with any other aspect of the business. But the feeling of satisfaction you get when you have your plan ready to execute is unlike anything else that you'll experience in the business.

It may feel as if you are lifting a massive weight from your shoulders… but be mindful, that weight can get dumped right back down onto you if you can't convince your entire team that the new plan is right for both them and the business.

Execution is the pillar considered to be the cornerstone of success and it's not something that you can do on your own.

Remember that getting buy-in from your team is a necessary first step to effective execution. If your team doesn't have the motivation to see your vision and drive change, your plans might fall through. This is why, as a leader, it's your job to unite the team under a common goal that they'll commit to fully, to pivot your hospitality business through the crisis!

Bear in mind that this is an ongoing process, as you can't just pitch the plan and expect everyone to carry it out. You must provide the tools, knowledge and motivation that your employees need.

When you make this happen, hold everyone accountable for the part that they'll play. Remember that your team looks up to you, so you must display this kind of accountability yourself.

And finally, don't let obstacles or seemingly viable new, trendy opportunities steer you off course. Have a clear goal, build a strategy for achieving it, and stay focused until you do.

CHAPTER NINE

# *Pillar #7 – Continue to Pivot and Make Changes Where Necessary*

In the previous chapter, I mentioned that pivoting isn't always a straight line. You'll have to make some adjustments along the way while sticking to the original plan. Plus, making long-term changes requires a big-picture approach. You can't just change one of your processes and think that you've pivoted.

Instead, you need to keep rethinking every aspect of your business and stay on the lookout for new pivots that are in line with your plan. To show you what this looks like in practice, I'd like to share some of the best pivots that Australian businesses have made recently.

## Rethinking the Dining Experience

As you read in Stephen Mercer's story, innovation can pay off handsomely. Stephen was one of the first hospitality business owners to popularise the at-home fine dining experience. Since then, many restaurants have pivoted to this model.

Venues such as Bentley Restaurant and Bar in Sydney launched their $110 takeaway box. The box didn't contain squashed hamburgers or soggy salads, but offered 13 packets that combined into a multi-course premium meal. Diners were delighted with everything required to make their food look and taste like it came straight from the chef's kitchen. Doing so involved giving the meals some finishing touches and diners would have to heat up the food, fluff the potatoes, or simply dress the salad. Bentley Restaurant and Bar was also listed on HungryHungry for pick up, drive-up and delivery.

Now, you might think that this is a bit counterintuitive. After all, when consumers go to a high-end restaurant, they do this because they want a particular experience. Having diners finalise the meals on their own could potentially ruin the experience venues spend time, energy and investment to create.

But the very opposite can be true as you pivot through a crisis. Encouraging those diners to give their dish a few finishing touches is closely related to the feeling of accomplishment and pride. At the same time, since they are not required to do any major work to finalise the dish, it's ready in no time, allowing them to enjoy a fine dining experience.

Plus, many savvy chefs and owners go beyond the cuisine and preparation instructions to make this happen. Bentley's owners also compiled a Spotify playlist that the customer could play at home. The playlist contained all the music you might hear in their restaurant to complement the fine foods and add to the overall unique dining experience.

Of course, many other restaurants executed the same idea in unique ways. Take CicciaBella Italian Osteria in Bondi Beach as an example. Before the restaurant reopened, head chef Mitch Orr wouldn't have much to do during the day. As a result, he decided to start creating online tutorials for some of the restaurant's most famous dishes.

In Orr's words:

*'I know people are panic buying pasta, minced beef and tomatoes, and that made me depressed because I could just imagine the terrible, terrible Bolognese people were cooking.'*

Orr's idea was very well-received by the online audience. With more free time, diners were willing and eager to learn how to cook some exclusive meals. For the most part, other restaurant owners and chefs who'd offered the same to their customers achieved positive results.

## Introducing Innovation

As takeout, self- and app-based delivery gained traction early in the pandemic crisis, hospitality business owners began finding new ways to offer more value to customers. They didn't have much choice, as the pandemic forced them to innovate quickly. Otherwise, they might've gone out of business.

Shane Delia, the owner of Maha in Melbourne, summarised the situation perfectly:

*'It hasn't really been good for a long time. We've been struggling, trying to make ends meet, keep people employed, become compliant, and do everything else, all with one of the lowest profit margins.'*

But Shane wasn't ready to let the pandemic ruin his business. He made a huge pivot towards bringing high-class dining experiences into diners homes. And that's how the idea of Providoor came to light.

Providoor lets customers order fine-dining takeout from some of the most exclusive restaurants with one day's notice. These include MoVida, Sunda, Flower Drum, Estelle, and of course, Maha.

The service adds value to customers way beyond the unique meals that it brings to their doorstep. For instance, there's an option to invite a chef to your home so that they can prepare the meal for you. Shane believes in this fantastic idea for dinner parties where the host doesn't want to spend precious time cooking. They have also added grocery, pre-mixed cocktails, kitchen items and gift cards.

Most importantly, Shane imagined Providoor as a long-term solution that the industry could benefit from.

*'Providoor is something that can get our restaurants through this mess, but also, potentially the next 15-20 years,'* he said. *'We want our restaurants to thrive, not just survive, because what is Australia without a strong hospitality industry.'*

This ties back perfectly to the point that I made in the previous chapter. Every pivot that you make should be the basis of the new way you'll do business in the long run. Rather than creating temporary solutions for an issue that a crisis brings, you should make viable long-term changes.

## Supporting the Industry

While the pandemic brought about many terrible stories of business closures, there was a silver lining to it. It strengthened the sense of community and encouraged people to start supporting one another. You could see examples of this all throughout the hospitality industry.

The Doughnut Department in Canberra was the personification of this. Owner Andrea Hutchinson shared a touching story from the period when her business was in danger. One day, a regular customer visited just for a coffee, and he insisted on paying $100. Reduced to tears, Hutchinson didn't want to accept the money, but the customer refused to take the change.

And while the Doughnut Department was forced to close temporarily through the crisis, the story proves several important points. First, it shows how valuable loyal customers are, which I've already highlighted. But also, it shows that customers are willing to come together in times of need and help local businesses out.

And it's far from the only feel-good story through the crisis. Dickson's popular Pho Phu Quoc, a family-run restaurant, started offering self-delivery for a number of reasons. They wanted to keep serving their customers while still keeping as many employees as possible in their jobs.

Sue Le, the owner of Dickson's, commented:

> *I am so devastated and heartbroken to see what is happening around the world. It was so terrible to let our staff go. And I am scared. But I'm also grateful to all the loyal customers who are trying to support us by putting in-home delivery orders during this time.*

This is how many hospitality business owners may feel during a crisis. While you'll certainly be afraid, you shouldn't let this fear consume you. Rather, you need to bravely take action and start pivoting.

However, this doesn't mean that you'll always get it right or that pivoting will work for your business. After all, failure is the worst fear of those who are trying to make meaningful changes. So, let me share one of the most valuable lessons that every hospitality business owner should know.

# *Don't Be Afraid to Throw in the Towel*

Every meaningful pivot idea involves a great deal of experimenting. No matter how good you are at planning, you'll likely see that there's a gap between theory and practice. As a result, you might make some mistakes that could discourage you.

However, you should never see failure as a reason to give up on growth. Just because something didn't work out, it does not mean everything will. Sometimes, you need to cut your losses and move on. I touched on this topic already, so I'd like to expand on it in this chapter.

Why?

Because giving up is the only true failure – everything else has a solution. In fact, failures can be an essential aspect of success. If you need proof, ask just about any person who's successful in business. No matter the industry, the most recognizable leaders are usually those who failed many times and learned from their mistakes.

To prove this, I'd like to share the stories of some of the world's most successful entrepreneurs. Each of them failed more than once before they made their mark in their industry.

## 1. Colonel Sanders

By now, it's impossible not to know of Colonel Sanders. He founded one of the world's best-known fast-food chains, Kentucky Fried Chicken (KFC).

Back when Colonel Sanders started his first restaurant, doing so was much harder than it is today. He didn't have the many tools that current business owners have at their fingertips. Instead, he had to take the old-fashioned route. He'd go door-to-door, pitching his ideas to anyone who'd listen.

However, he didn't have much luck. Colonel Sanders got rejected more than 1,000 times (1,009 according to certain reports). This was more than enough for most people to give up altogether.

But he never let this stand in his way. And there's no doubt that he was right not to quit. Eventually, his recipes got accepted by a restaurant outside of Utah. And today, KFC is well-known and loved by people across the globe. The company is worth a whopping US$8.5 billion, and it only keeps growing.

The lesson that Colonel Sanders' story can teach you is straightforward enough:

Perseverance pays off.

You'll want to remember this when pivoting your business. You might also face doubt, rejections, and other challenges when you start making big changes. But each of those challenges should serve as nothing but a stepping stone to success.

## 2. Henry Ford

As far as pivots go, there are very few industries as dynamic as the automotive industry. Imagine the kind of pivots that the industry's pioneer had to go through to make a name for himself.

Today, we remember Henry Ford as one of the most successful businessmen in history. But during his humble beginnings, very few saw him as such.

This would not have been that big an issue if Ford's investors weren't among those who doubted him. When he created his first automobile prototype, Ford needed a lot of external funding. He reached out to William H. Murphy, a businessman from Detroit. Murphy rounded up the shareholders and gave Ford a chance to produce his first car.

However, the production took longer than expected. Shareholders got anxious, stopped backing Ford, and the company got dissolved.

A few years later. Ford asked Murphy to give him a second chance. He'd learned from his initial failures and thought that he'd do better the second time around. Even though such second chances almost never happen in business, Ford got one from Murphy.

However, the second time was as big of a failure as the first. Ford felt pressured by Murphy yet again, so the partnership didn't work out.

It wasn't until two years later that Alexander Malcomson, a risk-hungry coal magnate, gave Ford all the freedom and capital that he needed. After recalibrating his business yet again. Ford introduced the Model A. And the rest is history. At the time when Ford died, his company was worth US$188 billion!

Ford's story is a perfect example of pivoting the right way. Sure, he made a lot of mistakes. And those mistakes cost him the trust of investors and much-needed funding. But he kept introducing one pivot after another. And with each new change, Ford armed himself with knowledge from the previous failure.

You need to do the exact same thing when pivoting your business. Instead of getting knocked down by failure, take it as a valuable lesson for moving forward. Keep experimenting, and use what you've learned to make each pivot better than the last one. Gradually, you'll get your business to wherever you want it to be.

## 3. Michael Jordan

If there's a person who sees failure the right way, it's Michael Jordan. Aside from being arguably the world's most successful basketball player, he's a prolific business owner. And in both basketball and business, Jordan has learned to understand and appreciate failure.

This might come as a surprise, but Jordan actually didn't make the varsity team in high school. For the longest time, there's been a rumour that he was cut from the team altogether. And while this isn't technically true, not making the team was certainly a major disappointment for the basketball legend.

Plus, it happened in the early days of his career. So many people would doubt themselves and give up in this situation. But Jordan's mindset didn't allow him to do this.

Even later in his career, Jordan has had many failures, despite being among the most lauded players of all-time. There's no better way to summarise them than by using his famous quote:

> *I have missed more than 9,000 shots in my career. I have lost almost 300 games. On 26 occasions I have been entrusted to take the game-winning shot, and I missed. I have failed over and over and over again in my life. And that is why I succeed.*

Pay attention to the last sentence here. Jordan said that he succeeded *because* of his failures, not *despite* them. And this is exactly why he's so successful in both basketball and in business. He understands that failure is an integral part of success. And so, should you.

Think of it this way:

The more you fail, the more lessons you'll learn. There's no better way to gain knowledge than by learning from your own experiences. And every successful person can tell you the same thing. As I mentioned, pivots are largely about experiments. You'll have to weed out all the ideas that don't work until you find what does.

## 4. Brian Chesky and Joe Gebbia

Airbnb is one of the most disruptive innovations in recent times. It transformed the accommodation industry and was one of the pioneers of the sharing economy. But this kind of success doesn't happen overnight, nor does it come without a few failures.

Before you learned about it, Airbnb was actually launched multiple times. And for the first few, it got pretty much no traction. The owners were sitting on a multibillion-dollar idea, and yet they were completely broke. Chesky and Gebbia were getting buried in debt and living on cereal.

It wasn't until they got accepted into Y Combinator that things started looking up. This exclusive start-up combinator offered the owners all the funding and mentorship they needed to pivot.

Little by little, Airbnb started dominating the accommodation industry. And at the time of writing, the company is worth approximately US$38 billion.

Airbnb started literally as an air mattress in a room that Chesky and Gebbia wanted to rent out to get by more easily. So not only did they start from the bottom, but they also faced many rejections before joining the Y Combinator. With proper guidance, the owners turned a few failed attempts into a mind-boggling success. What do you think is the most valuable takeaway from their story, aside from the importance of perseverance?

It's something that I talked about early in this book – finding a mentor. Aside from funding, the Y Combinator gave Chesky and Gebbia the guidance that they needed to make all the right changes to their platform. And the results were incredible.

By now, you already know the importance of having a mentor in times of crisis. Don't hesitate to ask for help when you see that things aren't working. Often, all you'll need will be a fresh pair of eyes to look at your plan.

Of course, you should be very careful in choosing the person whom you'll trust with providing this kind of guidance. Have a trusted advisor (or a few of them) and pivoting will be much easier. You'll handle failure the right way and see how you can come out on top the next time around.

# 5. Oprah Winfrey

Oprah Winfrey is undoubtedly one of the most influential people on the planet. Her show found its way into millions of homes across the globe. She has a loyal base of fans who listen to and trust her.

Imagine telling someone like her that she's not fit for TV. Well, that's exactly what her first boss told her. At the time, Oprah fought incredibly hard to land her first job as a news co-anchor. After overcoming everything from sexual abuse to racism, she found her way to the screen. Only for her boss to shut her down for 'being too vulnerable and emotional.'

Oprah's boss blamed her for the network's low ratings, and she got fired.

Not willing to let this discourage her, Oprah learned an invaluable lesson. She figured out that she didn't want to be a news anchor. She was much more interested in deep, personal stories. Once again, she fought against all the odds to land a job as a co-host on *People are Talking*.

For five years, the show performed extremely well. And then, Oprah got invited to become a host of a morning show in Chicago. The show ended up being a massive success, and so did Oprah.

Not long after that, Oprah decided to strike out on her own. And that's how the famous *Oprah Winfrey Show* was born. It went on to become one of the most successful talk shows in the history of television. As a result, Oprah became the highest-paying female entertainer of her time.

Today, Oprah owns her own network and has a personal net worth of US$2.6 billion. To say that her first boss was wrong would be a huge understatement.

As you can imagine, Oprah learned to deal with failure in a perfect way. Her own words can inspire you to do the same:

> *It doesn't matter how far you might rise. At some point, you are bound to stumble. If you're constantly pushing yourself higher and higher, the law of averages predicts that you will at some point fall. And when you do, I want you to remember this: There is no such thing as failure. Failure is just life trying to move us in another direction.*

Every word of this quote is absolutely right. As I noted already, success is largely a numbers game. And that's why it truly doesn't matter how many times you fail. You only need to do a few things right to pivot and achieve outstanding success.

## 6. Walt Disney

It's impossible to go through childhood without Disney. But aside from this, the company is a media titan with the kind of success that can be hard to comprehend. It's almost unfathomable to imagine such an industry giant struggling.

But before all the success, Walt Disney had to go through some incredibly tough times.

In 1920, he launched his first cartoon business with his brother. But only a couple of years later, the business went bankrupt. Disney decided to pivot and try to build a career as an actor. He travelled to Los Angeles in an attempt to make a name for himself. Unfortunately, this only resulted in more failures.

However, moving to Los Angeles was a blessing in disguise. Disney noticed that there was a massive gap in the market for animations. He called his brother to join him, and they founded an animation studio.

Remember Oswald the Lucky Rabbit? Probably not.

Well, it was Disney's first major success. But while he was away on a business trip, his producer took over his animations team. Worse yet, he robbed Disney of all the legal rights to his own creation.

Disney walked away and started over from scratch. While he was on the train to California, he created the famous Mickey Mouse. And from that point on, his business has seen a constant and steady rise. Of course, Disney remained an outstanding success long after its founder's death and is now worth a whopping US$130 billion.

It goes without saying that Disney learned how to rise up after getting knocked down. But his story teaches another invaluable lesson:

Failure might bring someone the most lucrative of opportunities.

If it wasn't for the failed business and acting career, Disney would've never moved to Los Angeles. And there's a high chance that the company would have ever been created.

So, when you face failure, do what Disney did and keep your eyes peeled for new opportunities. Keep your eye on the prize. You never know when the next one will bring outstanding success.

## *Embrace Failure*

I hope you can now see failure for what it truly is – a stepping stone to success. It's pretty much inevitable in any hospitality business, so you might as well choose to react to it in the right way. After all, the only option you ever have in life is how you'll react to what happens around you.

The stories you saw here prove how valuable failure is. And make no mistake – there are many stories about failures out there. There's rarely a self-made success without a few failures along the way.

So, when pivoting your business, welcome failure as a key pillar. Use it as an opportunity to learn something new. Don't try to fix what's clearly not working. Throw in the towel, learn from your mistakes, and then pivot again. The more you do it, the more chances you have of surviving and thriving through the crisis.

# CHAPTER TEN
# *It's Time to Make a Change*

I hope this book has changed the way you look at your hospitality business and how you will react during and after a crisis. I understand how terrifying it may feel to be exposed to circumstances outside your control. But this does not mean that you must be at the mercy of what happens around you.

By using what you've learned in this book, you'll be able to better control the situation of your business and make it more prepared in advance of future crises, and to help you survive and thrive. Feel free to return to this book whenever you need any guidance. While there are many ideas contained in this book that you can use, I'd like to go over the main takeaway that I want you to remember.

# *The Future Is in Your Hands*

Uncertainty can feel daunting and very uncomfortable. Each crisis disrupts the way you've operated your hospitality business in the past. Changing the course is challenging, and you'll likely feel tremendous pressure to do so as quickly as possible. You have much more control over the outcome than you might think.

It's not about what happens around you – it's about how you react to it. And hopefully, you are able to gain some insight from the many examples of successful pivots that you've read about in this book.

While some businesses may have closed under the pressure and uncertainty, many more have managed to pivot and position themselves for long-term survival. The category that you'll fall under depends solely on what you do.

In the words of Confucius:

*'He who says he can and he who says he can't, are both usually right.'*

This is a fundamental truth of business success. If you're in the right frame of mind, you'll keep finding new ways to pivot until you get it right.

## *Learn to Appreciate Failure*

I have made mistakes that I learned a great deal from to get to where I am today and revealed just a few examples. And yet, I managed to climb my way up the industry.

My journey has been a long and exciting one, with many twists and turns. And yours will be as well. But that doesn't mean that you'll always get it right. You'll have to do a lot of experimenting until you find what works in the long run. You must welcome the opportunity to make mistakes and learn from them.

After all, this is what continuous progress is all about. You try something new, mess up, learn the lesson, and hopefully do better the next time. This is how you fill your life as a hospitality business owner with an abundance of experiences that will get you to where you want to be. There are very few things as valuable as experience.

# *Choose Your People Wisely*

For whatever reason, many hospitality business owners continue to believe that the road to success is a lonely one. If you're among them, you may need to let go of this kind of thinking. Trying to do it all alone isn't only unnecessary, but also counterproductive to your success. No person is an island.

Why struggle to juggle all your challenges when there are people who can take a lot off your plate? Especially when those people are experts that already have the knowledge that you're still yet to gain.

For this reason, surrounding yourself with a group of capable people is critical to success. You need to find those who've already gone through similar situations and have them show you the way. Mentorship can be a massive shortcut to minimise the trial-and-error period and get you to the desired outcome much quicker.

So, if you haven't already, find a mentor with your business' best interests in mind. Reach out to trusted advisors and don't hesitate to ask for help. Your competition will certainly take advantage of this, so you don't want to fall behind.

# *Get to Know Your Business*

Even though many people can help you and provide the guidance that you need, you're the one calling the shots. No one cares about your business more than you do, and it's your responsibility to ensure it survives and thrives, especially during a crisis.

Because of this, you must know your business better than your mentors, employees, and all other stakeholders.

Don't forget, change starts with your financials. They're the only thing that presents a clear picture of how well you've done so far. So, get good at understanding and managing the numbers.

When you make this happen, you'll have much more clarity as to where your business needs to go. You'll use those numbers for the forecasts and plans that will be your solid guide to pivot. If the data that you build a plan around is faulty, your strategy will be as well. You might take your business in the wrong direction and damage it further.

So, don't simply delegate all your financials to an accountant. While they'll be the one crunching the numbers, you'll have to make decisions based on them. So, get involved in those few critical reports, and you'll have a firm grasp on your hospitality business.

# *Don't Stop Evolving*

A crisis shouldn't be the only time when you decide to make a change. Rather, this should be something that you do on a continuous basis. The hospitality industry shifts and evolves constantly. If you're standing still, you're actually moving backwards. You risk falling behind the innovative trends that define the new rules of success.

This is why you must keep your eyes peeled for new opportunities and pivots. At the very least, you need to keep up with the market, or better yet, innovate and be one step ahead of the competition.

In this book, hopefully, you have learned what it takes to make this happen. Now, it's time to put this knowledge to good use. So, get out there, follow these 7 Pillars to Pivoting Your Business Through a Crisis, and drive your business towards a more successful future! And don't forget to 'Keep your eye on the prize'.

# *Resources:*

https://www.abc.net.au/news/science/2020-03-05/bushfire-crisis-five-big-numbers/12007716

https://www.abc.net.au/news/2020-02-19/australia-bushfires-how-heat-and-drought-created-a-tinderbox/11976134?nw=0

http://climatecollege.unimelb.edu.au/recent-australian-droughts-may-be-worst-800-years

https://www.abc.net.au/news/drought/

https://www.theguardian.com/australia-news/2020/apr/07/coronavirus-crisis-has-had-staggering-impact-on-australian-businesses-data-reveals

https://www.abc.net.au/radio/programs/pm/recovery-for-restaurants-and-cafes-expected-to-take-years/12245186

https://www.inc.com/john-rampton/10-reasons-why-a-mentor-is-a-must.html

https://www.entrepreneur.com/article/280134

https://www.sba.gov/blog/mentoring-missing-link-small-business-growth-survival

https://www.theupsstore.com/about/pressroom/small-business-mentoring-month-2014

https://mentorloop.com/blog/what-mentoring-is-not/

https://www.nytimes.com/2009/12/23/dining/23menus.html

https://www.touchbistro.com/blog/how-to-calculate-your-restaurants-prime-costs/

https://www.lightspeedhq.com.au/blog/complete-guide-to-restaurant-profit-margins/

https://www.adelaidenow.com.au/delicious-sa/adelaide-restaurants-and-hotels-beg-for-local-support-as-they-get-hit-by-downturn-in-trade/news-story/c335504c2f1d1a4815cbaf6128ab8c1a

https://www.business.qld.gov.au/running-business/finances-cash-flow/managing-money/break-even-point

https://www.fool.com/the-blueprint/profit-and-loss-statement/

https://issuu.com/engagemedia/docs/r_c_july_2011

https://smallbusiness.chron.com/importance-profit-loss-table-64761.html

https://fitsmallbusiness.com/profit-and-loss-statement-pl-income/

https://www.franchisebusiness.com.au/gfc-proves-a-winner-for-fast-food-franchises/

https://www.salesforce.com/au/blog/2017/11/9-sales-forecasting-tips-for-small-business.html

https://saaslist.com/blog/small-business-sales-forecast/

https://www.inc.com/guides/2010/12/7-tips-for-business-forecasting.html

https://www.maguiretraining.co.uk/blog/7-tips-to-improve-your-business-forecasting

https://www.businessgrowthservices.co/why-is-financial-forecasting-so-critical-for-your-business/

https://www.accountingdepartment.com/blog/ten-ways-to-improve-your-budgeting-forcasting

https://www.couriermail.com.au/lifestyle/food/qld-taste/adapt-or-die-restaurant-sectors-starkchoice/news-story/e25fc1ac843ba5931e1a15b0c2206199

https://www.theaustralian.com.au/life/food-drink/coronavirus-pull-your-head-in-restaurateur-slaps-down-critics/news-story/50aa00f07265802a91ef06847fe55ebc

https://www.theage.com.au/national/victoria/a-night-out-at-home-how-melbourne-s-restaurants-are-adapting-to-restrictions-20200416-p54kj8.html

https://www.healthline.com/health/how-long-does-it-take-to-form-a-habit#takeaway

https://www.abc.net.au/radio/programs/am/restaurants-look-to-takeaway-amid-coronavirus-slowdown/12062054

https://www.mybusiness.com.au/management/6756-restaurants-seek-rent-abatement-uber-eats-waives-delivery-fees

https://www.fastcasual.com/articles/7-technologies-transforming-the-restaurant-industry/

https://www.ezcater.com/lunchrush/restaurant/7-step-guide-creating-restaurant-marketing-plan-drives-business/

https://pos.toasttab.com/blog/restaurant-marketing-plan

https://www.goodfood.com.au/eat-out/news/cutprice-corona-and-homedelivered-steaks-how-sydney-restaurants-are-responding-to-the-covid-crisis-20200317-h1mlrx

https://www.afr.com/work-and-careers/workplace/restaurants-gain-workplace-flexibility-in-shift-to-delivery-model-20200330-p54f7q

https://www.smh.com.au/business/small-business/blindly-hoping-for-the-best-restaurants-take-precautions-20200518-p54u19.html

https://www.smh.com.au/business/small-business/restaurants-go-it-alone-despite-deliveroo-and-uber-eats-fee-reductions-20200511-p54ruy.html

https://www.goodfood.com.au/eat-out/news/from-whole-chooks-to-caviar-discounted-restaurant-produce-hits-sydneys-retail-market-20200327-h1my65

https://www.unileverfoodsolutions.com.au/chef-inspiration/fighting-covid-19-together/eatalonetogether-to-rally-support-for-aussie-restaurants-and-cafes/eatalonetogether-home-delivery-and-takeaway-movement-to-support-local-australian-restaurants.html

https://maharestaurant.com.au/whatson/cooking-classes-with-shane-delia/

https://www.inc.com/elizabeth-dukes/4-strategies-for-getting-employees-excited-about-change.html

https://www.forbes.com/sites/brentgleeson/2016/10/17/8-steps-for-helping-your-employees-accept-change/#703d4b1e29f2

https://www.bizjournals.com/bizjournals/how-to/growth-strategies/2015/03/5-top-ways-to-implement-a-strategic-plan.html

https://www.rootinc.com/blog/successful-change-management-9-tips/

https://blog.capterra.com/fool-proof-tactics-to-get-employees-onboard-with-organizational-change/

https://www.iofficecorp.com/blog/changing-your-workplace-strategy-how-to-get-employees-onboard

https://www.abc.net.au/news/2020-04-25/chef-cooked-meals-as-takeaway-amid-coronavirus-lockdown/12181842

https://www.smartcompany.com.au/coronavirus/atlas-dining-pivot-covid-19/

https://hercanberra.com.au/life/business-career/online-perish-business-pivots-around-corona/

https://www.broadsheet.com.au/sydney/guides/live-list-sydney-restaurants-pivoting-takeaway

https://www.delicious.com.au/eat-out/article/premium-food-delivery-service-providoor-launches-melbourne-sydney/jw7j22q1

https://propertyupdate.com.au/six-famous-people-who-failed-before-succeeding/

https://smallbiztrends.com/2016/01/entrepreneurs-who-failed.html

https://small-bizsense.com/10-famous-entrepreneurs-who-failed-in-business-before-becoming-successful/

https://www.lenovys.com/en/blog/airbnbs-story-teaches-how-to-make-mistakes-in-a-planned-manner/

https://www.thejobnetwork.com/how-oprah-winfrey-overcame-failure/

https://www.intellectualventures.com/buzz/insights/failing-for-success-henry-a.-ford

www.ingramcontent.com/pod-product-compliance
Lightning Source LLC
Chambersburg PA
CBHW071511150426
43191CB00009B/1491